Life Drawing

Life Drawing

Perception and Practice

RONALD CLARK

*

'The fringèd curtains of thine eye advance,
And say what thou seest yond.'

from *The Tempest*

STUDIO
VISTA

Studio Vista
an imprint of
Cassell
Wellington House, 125 Strand
London WC2R 0BB

First published 1995

British Library Cataloguing in Publication Data
A catalogue record for this book is available from the British Library

ISBN 0 289 801 427

Distributed in the United States by
Sterling Publishing Co., Inc.
387 Park Avenue South
New York, NY 10016-8810

Distributed in Australia by
Capricorn Link (Australia) Pty Ltd
2/13 Carrington Road
Castle Hill, NSW 2154

Typeset by Ronald Clark

Printed in Spain

Contents

Preface

The origins of this book go back some years to when I first began to teach life drawing. My class was part of the excellent, but unhappily now diminishing, local authority adult education provision whose roots in the UK go back to the turn of the century when the Workers' Educational Association was formed. My predecessors had taught life drawing and painting continuously in the same building since the 1920s, which gives some idea of the strength of demand there is, and always has been, for this activity.

During the course of my teaching I began to record any pertinent remarks I made in my earnest endeavour to stimulate my students. I found I was also recalling phrases and theories that had first fired my imagination as an art student in the mid-1950s. Much of the thinking and structure of this material has been prompted by the enthusiasm and loyalty of my students; their dedication to the subject has been a powerful stimulant for me. I would like to express my sincere gratitude to them in equal measure to my own tutors from those distant halcyon days.

I would also like to thank my wife Stella for her encouragement, confidence and continued support during the long period of this book's preparation. Finally, I am greatly indebted to Billie Figg for reading my manuscript and suggesting so many worthwhile improvements.

I hope this book may help to open the eyes of many more potential artists. Although it cannot teach them how to draw, I believe it could begin to teach them how to see.

R.C.

London

A drawing which contains many of the subject heads of this book including stance, form, weight, perspective, foreshortening, viewpoint, colour, lighting, composition and spatial awareness. (*Pastels 23 x 17 in/58.5 x 43 cm*)

Introduction
ATTITUDE AND APTITUDE

'All our knowledge has its origins in our perceptions.' – Leonardo da Vinci

Life drawing is a practice which is complete in itself – absorbing and infinitely rewarding. For the beginner who has had no previous practical experience it can become a passport into a world of wonder; or it can be the means of regeneration for the artist who has been drawing for more than fifty years. There is no restriction as to who may participate, an artistic gift or aptitude is not essential and there is no failure except in no longer trying. The only requirements are an open, enquiring mind and a tenacious but humble attitude. Yet for 25 years life drawing was out of fashion among the art school fraternity where conceptual art reigned, the movement which denounced all traditional artistic values by claiming that concepts alone were all important and could be expressed through a multiplicity of media including photographs, film, video, documents and language. Now, however, life drawing has once more been universally recognized as containing the roots of every single visual application from painting to illustration, from sculpture to fashion, from printmaking to cartoons. Strangely, outside the art schools, among the often derided 'amateur' students attending adult education classes, it continued to be practised and remained extremely popular throughout this period of relegation.

The nude form, male or female, young or old, presents the artist with an infinite number of problems of perception to solve, as well as the greatest variety of ideas he or she could ever need or wish to have to stimulate their visual imagination. Each time we draw from the nude we are confronted with trying to comprehend the questions of stance, proportion, form, weight, texture, perspective, pattern, harmony and space: all of them fascinating enigmas, and all of them waiting to be found during the engaging and challenging quest of 'learning to see', for art is the difference between seeing and merely identifying.

The nude form presents the artist with an infinite number of problems of perception to solve. (*Pastels 14 x 10 in/35.5 x 25.5 cm*)

The act of drawing from nature, more especially from a life model, is a voyage of discovery and detection. Each new drawing should be a fresh investigation, a totally new adventure, and not simply a repetition of one that has been made several times before. Each journey is uncharted until you begin to ask yourself questions. The more questions you ask and attempt to solve with the aid of the tools and materials at your disposal, the greater the scope there will be for further revelations because every question tackled encourages more and more exploration, and each discovery increases the enjoyment. The whole process is self-perpetuating and continuous. Every single pose of every single model is unique, so you cannot place any reliance on work you may have done in the past. Every drawing is a wholly new beginning. Come to it fresh each time with an enquiring and open mind and you will be rewarded by seeing something – perhaps a delicate relationship of texture or colour, a subtlety of form, a single exquisite feature – that you have never noticed before; a totally new experience which, if you are true to the sensation of the moment, will become manifest in the finished drawing.

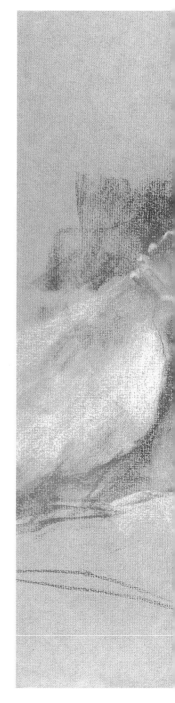

Forget yesterday's drawing, or last week's. This is happening now and every stroke is a new beginning, another chance to take a step forward. Just immerse yourself in the quest and as you proceed, sometimes tentatively, sometimes vigorously, step by step, inch by inch, progress is made. Accept that you have never seen exactly this pose before; you have never wholly experienced this visual sensation before; you have never made precisely this statement before. Expel all other matters from your mind. There is only *now*, no future, no past, just this very minute and only you and your subject and your drawing matter – nothing else exists. Occasionally one's attention is drawn to an aspect of the subject that is of such exquisite delicacy that breathing itself has to be suspended for a moment in order to achieve any approximation of its form on paper. Once you enter this state of absorption and depth of involvement, you will begin to understand the attraction and the true rewards of this wonderful pursuit.

Try to think beyond the prosaic desire to render a likeness. Drawing is not a matter of mere copying, for copying can be equated with reciting a poem without showing any evidence that the content has been either understood or appreciated. Photographic verisimilitude is not a particularly worthy ambition for the draughtsman. Drawing and

Every pose of every model
is unique, so each drawing
is a new beginning. (*Pastels
13 x 19 in/33 x 48 cm*)

photography differ in a number of ways – one being that of selectivity. It is not necessary to draw every tiny detail, every fold of skin and every fingernail or eyelash in order to appreciate and express your feeling about your subject. The art is in the seeing, selecting and emphasizing whatever features excite your interest at the time.

Of course a photographer also has a choice. He will choose his subject, the lighting, aperture and the time exposure, but then he can only influence his picture further – and then only to a limited degree – through the developing and masking process. The draughtsman on the other hand can select and emphasize – even distort – any aspect of his subject he wishes at any time, a process which continues right up to the end of the drawing session. Whether photography may or may not be art, art is not photography.

Some of the finest old master draughtsmen – Hans Holbein in sixteenth-century England, for example, and Ingres in early nineteenth-century France – refined their drawing techniques to such a degree that only the finest of lines, the most delicate of statements were visible. But these marks contained as much information as many more detailed executions might have done. This was not simply a technical manipulation of the materials, but the result of profound understanding and selectivity. It came only after years of dedicated effort and enquiry, delving deeply into their art by challenging their own powers of perception and becoming more and more discriminatory. Holbein was not only able to depict his sitter's lips and mouth in the thinnest of delicate lines imaginable, but in so doing he recreated the whole of the surrounding part of the face as well. There is no tonal difference between the background paper and that of the flesh, yet, because the artist has felt the distinction so vividly, one knows instinctively that the cheek and upper lip are soft but solid flesh while the background is merely a void. If it can be said that there is an element of magic in drawing, it is surely to be found here. No photograph has ever achieved as much.

'Less is more' is a phrase frequently heard in the tuition of drawing to encourage more precise selectivity. It is applicable, though, only after a great deal of experience in the art. Some artists of the modern period – Picasso and Matisse, for example – were able to reduce the execution of their drawings to the most basic of simple elements – a pen and ink outline or a silhouette ink-blob – but from the hand of a genius these unadorned statements are capable of conveying infinite power, rapid movement or sublime beauty, and sometimes even wit.

In practical terms, ask yourself why you are rendering this particular shadow or that item of background. Are these elements *essential* to your understanding of the pose or to your expression of it? School yourself to think in the simplest, most direct statements. It is often the big sweeping application of line or tone that best captures the essence of a pose. And be conscious of when enough is enough. Avoid over-refinement and be content to achieve one thing at a time and not expect to become a master overnight. Occasionally, each one of us experiences that 'happy accident' when an unintentional mark or smudge succeeds in revealing some aspect of the subject which all our deliberate marks have failed to do. Recognition of this providence is part of the understanding. Accept it and pass on to the next challenge. As Albert Einstein said in a somewhat different context, the important thing is not to stop questioning.

Finally, let us dispel any misunderstandings that might still exist in some minds with regard to the nature of nudity. I suppose even in this modern and permissive age there could be some slight embarrassment for the new student initially confronting their first nude model. No doubt among the young it may even cause a little nervous giggling. In my experience this lasts for about five minutes before the purpose and objectives of the class take hold. At the beginning of his great book, *The Nude*, the late Kenneth Clark makes the following observation:

> The English language, with its elaborate generosity, distinguishes between the naked and the nude. To be naked is to be deprived of our clothes, and the word implies some of the embarrassment most of us feel in that condition. The word "nude", on the other hand, carries, in educated usage, no uncomfortable overtone. The vague image it projects into the mind is not of a huddled and defenceless body, but of a balanced, prosperous, and confident body: the body re-formed. In fact, the word was forced into our vocabulary by critics of the early eighteenth century to persuade the artless islanders that, in countries where painting and sculpture were practised and valued as they should be, the naked human body was the central subject of art.

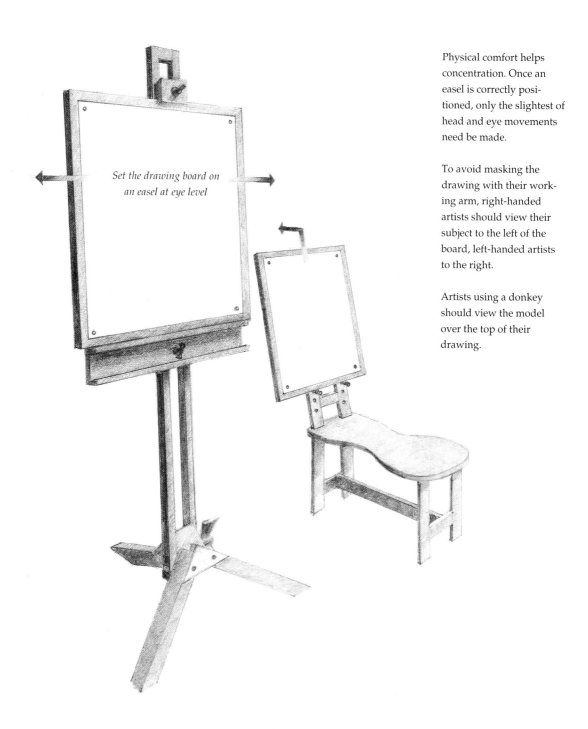

*Set the drawing board on
an easel at eye level*

Physical comfort helps concentration. Once an easel is correctly positioned, only the slightest of head and eye movements need be made.

To avoid masking the drawing with their working arm, right-handed artists should view their subject to the left of the board, left-handed artists to the right.

Artists using a donkey should view the model over the top of their drawing.

Part 1
STRUCTURE AND DEFINITION

'The beauty in a picture does not really lie in the beauty of its subject matter.'
– E.H. Gombrich

A question often asked by students new to a life class is 'Where do I begin a drawing?' The honest answer is that it does not really matter. There may be a number of considerations which could influence the starting point, such as how long the pose is to be held, or whether a specific theme has been set as an exercise. Otherwise the choice is highly individual. Some artists feel that the basic structure or stance needs to be established first, while others are compelled to begin with the head. One point that should always be borne in mind is the size and shape the drawing will occupy on the paper. Some basic pre-planning is advisable.

Planning and Building

When it is intended to draw from a single pose over an extended period, say two hours or longer, the approach to the drawing can be more planned and structured than is otherwise possible to achieve over a much shorter period. With this amount of time, attention can be paid to preparing the groundwork, giving careful consideration to the viewpoint, the composition, the size of your drawing relative to the paper, the medium and the materials you elect to use. Then, like an architect creating the design for a building, plan the basic framework first and build gradually step by step. By carefully establishing a number of individual points of reference and the relationships between them – rather like plotting the co-ordinates of a map – you will be able to build the whole figure progressively upon the foundations and the internal scaffolding. Take your time and do not feel you have to rush at getting a result.

When working at an easel, your eye level should be about one-third down from the top of the board. If you are right-handed, position the easel and board in such a way that the model can be viewed immediately to the left of your drawing (to the right for left-handed people). This will allow you to see clearly without the drawing arm crossing your line of vision. The less head movement there is between looking at the model and looking at the drawing, the less demand there will be to carry the information in the memory. The ideal is to be able to see the model and the drawing almost at the same time. If you are drawing seated on a wooden donkey, make sure you can see comfortably over the top of your board.

Having first positioned your sheet of paper appropriate to the pose (vertically for a standing or seated pose, horizontally for a reclining one), determine the centre point of the figure roughly and show this in the centre of your paper. Then fix the extremities at four points reasonably close to the edges but allowing a little room for adjustments. Quite often, due to a lack of preparation and foresight, inexperienced draughtsmen discover that, after working at their drawing for some time, it is either running off one edge or it appears uncomfortably off-centre.

Be prepared to introduce whatever aids help you to observe your subject more precisely and more intensely. For example, by cutting out a small rectangular frame from card or thick paper through which to view the pose, you can get a feeling of how best to position your drawing on the paper. This viewing frame may also be used to check the vertical and horizontal alignments of any two or more features. A decorators' plumb-line and bob is another device which, when held out at arm's length and viewed with one eye, can also be used to check which contours or features are vertical and any that appear one above another.

You can also adopt the time-honoured measuring technique of holding out a pencil at arm's length, closing one eye, and then by using the pencil as a gauge and sliding the thumb down from one end as the marker, calculate and compare two relative measurements. It is essential to keep your arm out straight, otherwise the compared elements will not be of equal value. Estimate how many times the width of the body goes into the height of a standing figure, or into the height from the top of the head to the base of the spine of a seated figure. Alternatively, having measured the distance between the top of the head and the chin, find two other points of reference that have the same measurement. It may be the distance between the the two shoulders or between one shoulder and the elbow on the same side. Make simple marks at these points of

Visual measurements should be made by comparing the distance between comparative points of reference:

A—A width of head = width of left buttock;

B—B width across shoulders goes four times into height of figure;

C—C width across knees = shoulder to elbow = arm joint to pelvis;

D—D base of neck to crotch = crotch to ankle.

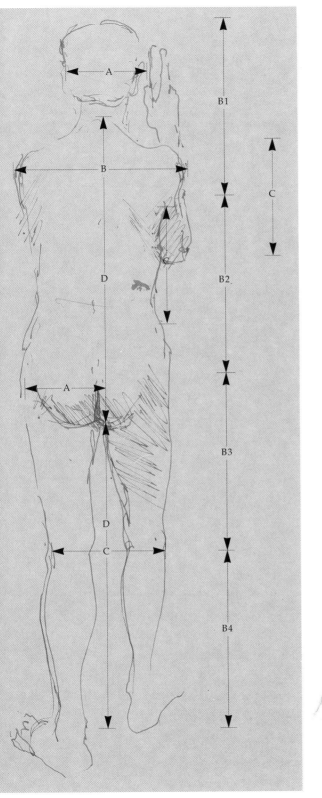

A pencil can be used as a gauge by holding it at arm's length and estimating comparative measurements with the thumb.

A card frame and plumbline can be used as aids to accurate alignment.

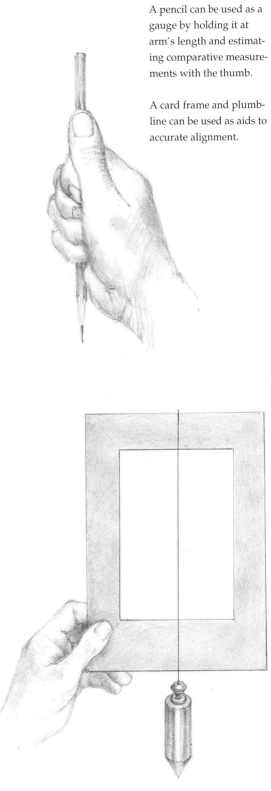

Choose clearly defined
measuring points and
continue checking and
re-checking them as the
drawing evolves.
(*Monochrome wash
17 x 12 in/43 x 30.5 cm*)

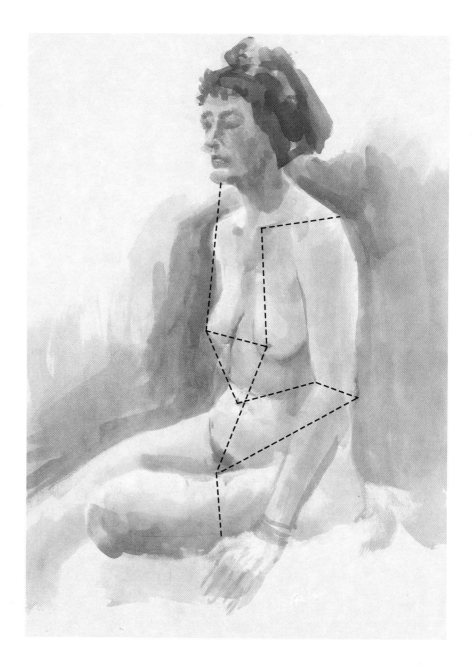

reference, changing their position as often as you need to make adjustments. Plot as many comparative measurements as you can both before and during the execution of your drawing, increasing their number gradually until you have a good overall set of comparisons.

As you build your drawing in this carefully structured way, it will lead you into seeing and feeling with more intensity the stance, the form and the weight of the figure. Look for the internal thrust of the limbs and

The direction and structure of the spinal column and the thrust of the limbs should be the first points to look for. (*Pen and wash highlighted with white chalk 17 x 13 in/43 x 33 cm*)

spinal column and ask yourself the fundamental questions about balance and stress. And by choosing not to follow the contours slavishly as though there were universal laws dictating that you must only fill in the substance of the figure once the outline has been completed, you will begin to understand more about the living forces that make up the human frame. Of course, the contours – that outer shape we see which visually separates the figure from its background – are of profound importance in drawing, but they can only be fully appreciated after coming to terms with the inner content.

Be sure you only draw what you see and not what you think you know. This can only be achieved by looking intensely at the model for at least the same length of time as you focus your eyes on your drawing. Some draughtsmen claim that the time ratio should be 60:40, or even 70:30, in favour of looking at the model. Between focusing on the model and looking at the paper, a good deal of memorizing is involved and this will be better served by concentrated observation than by superficial glances every now and again.

Constantly check and correct the marks you make. Never be ashamed of either making mistakes or showing your corrections. And beware the fear of failure. Remember the well-founded maxim, 'The man who never made a mistake never made anything.' It is only by leaving the previous marks where you can see them as you review your work and redraw parts of it, that you will have any record of the improvements you make.

It is important to work through and draw over mistakes, continually reworking the form and correcting relationships. (*Sepia wash, pencil and ink 11 x 16 in/28 x 40.5 cm*)

The exercise is not to produce neat and tidy pictures but to develop a penetrating analytical vision.

Because there is a danger of the continuous reworking becoming too dark and eventually unworkable, it is wise not to start off with too heavy a treatment. A light touch does not necessarily mean a tentative one; you can be as direct and positive with a faint mark as you can with a blacker one. Be convinced of the rightness of the mark you make but then be equally critical of it once you have made it and, as you look again and again at the model, be prepared to alter what you have done as often as is necessary. Those who are familiar with the drawings of Leonardo da Vinci will know that, together with many meticulously finished examples, there are some that are worked over and over in the attempt to master accuracy of observation and composition.

Wherever possible, the use of an eraser should be avoided. Firstly, because rubbing out is a negative and destructive action whereas drawing should be positive and constructive; secondly, the marks you make are your signposts telling you where you have come from and, if you erase your work, you lose sight of the route you have taken on your journey. If the drawing is becoming too dark and unworkable, use the eraser only to 'ghost' it down without obliterating the marks altogether. As you become a more experienced draughtsman, you may be able to develop the use of the eraser as a positive implement and actually 'draw' with it on to a darkened or smudgy area in a constructive way. This is particularly appropriate for charcoal drawings. Generally though, to begin with, the eraser should not be needed.

If at some stage of your drawing you are convinced there are many aspects of it that are wrong and yet you do not know where to begin to put them right, try to identify one small area or detail that you are reasonably content with and use it as the focal point from which to rebuild the rest. Allow the drawing to grow outwards from this point by measuring a number of other features from it. Choose measuring points that are clearly focused and sharply delineated: for example, a bone like the knee-cap or elbow which shows on the surface of the form, or surface features such as the nipples or the navel which are small enough to be pinpointed, or wherever the tightness of a fold in the flesh creates a clear line, as happens between the buttocks or beneath the armpits. As you measure and relate these elements to both that feature originally selected and to each other, then the redrawing of the figure will develop with increasing accuracy.

An example showing how, in some reclining poses, the ribcage may be positioned at one angle while the pelvis is at another. (*Black and white pastels 11 x 14 in/28 x 35.5 cm*)

PLANNING AND BUILDING – SUMMARY

- *Plan the size of your drawing by marking off the four extremities.*
- *Plot comparative measurements throughout your drawing.*
- *Focus your attention on the model for at least as long as you look at your drawing.*
- *Progress from light marks to dark ones.*
- *Avoid rubbing out and benefit from being able to see your mistakes.*

Proportion and Sight Size

For a student just beginning the multi-faceted study of life drawing, it may be advisable to tackle first attempts at 'sight size'. This is the term used to describe a life study which is drawn to the same size as the pose is viewed. The laws of perspective dictate that this will vary in direct relation to your viewing distance from the model: the closer you stand, the larger it will appear. Its value to the inexperienced draughtsman is that any visual measurements made by the method described under Planning and Building, pages 16–18, provided they conform to a consistent method of calculation, can be precisely translated to the paper.

If your paper is positioned at roughly arm's length away from you, then all measurements taken at arm's length can be accurately plotted on to it. First, look carefully at the model and select one longish element such as the head, arm, thigh or shoulders. Now hold out a pencil at arm's length as described above, close one eye, visually fix the end at some point on the body and slide the thumb down from one end of the pencil until it corresponds to the length of the selected feature. Without moving your thumb, lay the pencil on to the paper at roughly the correct angle of stance and make two marks to plot the length. Repeat this technique for various other parts of the figure and keep checking relative measurements throughout the progress of your drawing. The consequent image that you build up will be shown at sight size.

Stance and Balance

The first point to observe when beginning to tackle any drawing of the human figure is the basic stance of the pose. Take a good look at the overall posture and decide which are the vertical stresses most involved in retaining support and balance. To begin with, ignore subtleties of texture and detail – or even form – but concentrate instead on searching out the essential structure. This can be especially important when a limited time-scale has been set. The shorter the time available to complete a drawing, the more essential it is to capture the character of the whole posture swiftly.

When the model has his or her weight unevenly distributed – on one

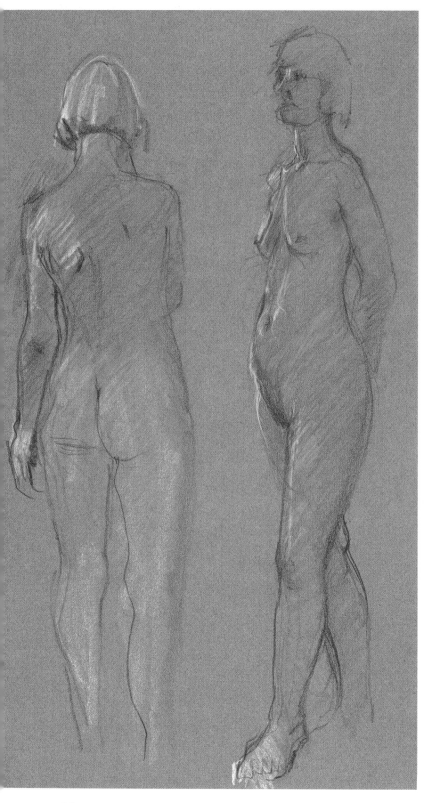

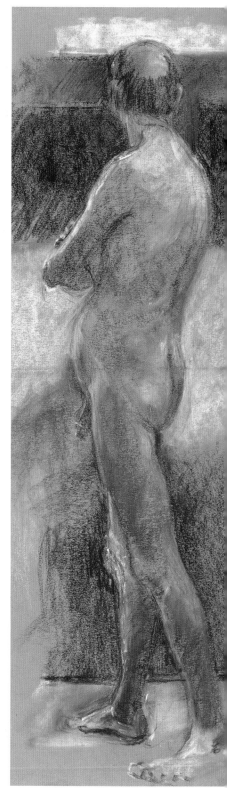

Standing poses are governed by the spinal column and the distribution of weight through the pelvis and the legs. (*Left sanguine, brown and white pencils 19 x 12 in/48 x 30.5 cm; right pastels 20 x 9 in/51 x 23 cm*)

foot more than the other – observe how the pelvis tilts, making the hip of the standing leg protrude and lift, and how the buttock contracts to take the strain. See also how the shoulders and ribcage invariably seem to counterbalance this by sloping in the opposite direction. Take note also how the head is set directly above the standing foot to ensure the model's balance is maintained.

Similar movements which enable balanced and reasonable comfort for the model can also be seen in seated and reclining poses. For instance, if body weight is being supported on one arm, the shoulder rises to take the strain. In a relaxed seated position as opposed to an upright one, watch for how the spine curves back from the pelvis and forward again at the shoulders. When the model is in a turned position, notice where the rotation originates: the pelvis remains facing the original direction but the ribcage and shoulders face another. The neck and the head are a continuation of the spinal column and should not be separately portrayed except when the head is being drawn by itself. The whole frame of the the body is conditioned and supported by the spinal column, so it therefore helps to establish the pose by featuring this early on in your drawing. Attempt to identify and position the curving line of the spine even if it may not be entirely visible from your viewpoint. If you have a fully frontal view, imagine where and how the spinal column relates to that part of the body you can see. Not only will this help to reveal basic essentials about the pose, but it will also help to encourage you to think and draw in terms other than contours.

Never hesitate to take a look at the model from other angles in order to satisfy yourself that you understand exactly how the pose is constructed. It often helps to see the pose from another angle to clarify any parts that seem uncertain from only one. A limb seen from your viewpoint in a foreshortened way can be better understood when it is also looked at from one or both sides.

There are any number of stress and balance points to look for and which help to reveal the basic posture. If you imagine you were in the pose yourself, it will help to indicate where these are. Ask yourself: where are the pressure points? which muscles are absorbing the strain? which parts of the body are tense and which relaxed? Once you begin to envisage and appreciate these pressures for yourself, you will be in a more receptive frame of mind to interpret them in your drawing.

STANCE AND BALANCE – SUMMARY

- *Look for the vertical stresses that support a standing pose.*
- *Identify which foot is taking the weight.*
- *See whether the shoulders slope to counterbalance the pelvic tilt.*
- *Note the position of the head above the standing foot.*
- *In a reclining pose, observe how the shoulder of the supporting arm rises.*
- *Trace the spinal column right through from head to pelvis.*
- *View the model from other angles for a better understanding.*
- *Think yourself into the pose in order to appreciate the points of stress.*

Left The spine rotates to such a degree that the shoulders can be seen at right-angles to the pelvis. (*Pastels 16 x 9 in/ 40.5 x 23 cm*)

Right Awareness of the negative shapes helps the drawing of limbs in proportion to the torso. (*Pastels 19 x 13 in/48 x 33 cm*)

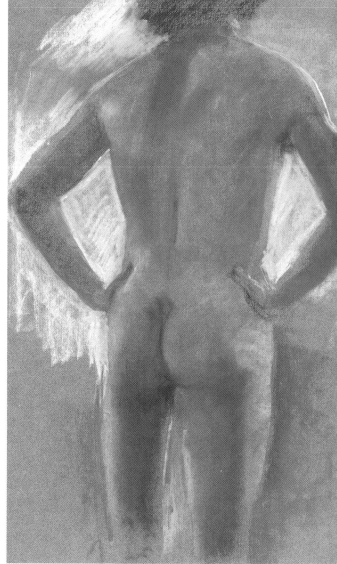

Negative Shapes

If the shapes formed by the posed model might best be described as the positive design or composition, the holes and gaps in between the limbs and other parts of the body are known as 'negative shapes'. This term is adopted not because it refers to any rigid definition of blackness but merely because it represents the opposite to the positive nature of the figure itself. In fact, so-called negative shapes can be of any tone or any colour.

When trying to establish proportion, stance and balance in your drawing, these negative shapes are ideal points of reference. For example, if the figure has the hands on the hips and you suspect you have drawn the torso too long in comparison to the arms, look closely at the negative shape framed by the arm and the body. Decide if the triangle is equal on all sides, equal on two sides or with all sides different. By turning your attention to the negative shapes, they will assist you in making adjustments to the positive form.

Once you are accustomed to looking for the negative shapes, you will become conscious of seeing them in many other places, not just where the background shows through but also where other parts of the body appear. As in some modern sculptures, the empty spaces become just as significant as the solid forms surrounding them.

Form and Texture

The human body is three-dimensional. It is not a flat, cut-out shape but has volume both in the whole figure and in its individual parts – the torso, the head and the limbs. Drawing is to some extent the translation of that three-dimensional solidity on to a two-dimensional surface. Try to envisage what you could see of the depth from front to back if the model were made from transparent glass. Observe how each part of the body relates to every other part, not simply as shapes across a frontal plane but also one in front of the other in space. Look for planes created by flattish areas such as the chest, back and abdomen; but also the less obvious planes like that created invisibly across the lap of a seated model. Try to express the three-dimensional directions of these simplified planes.

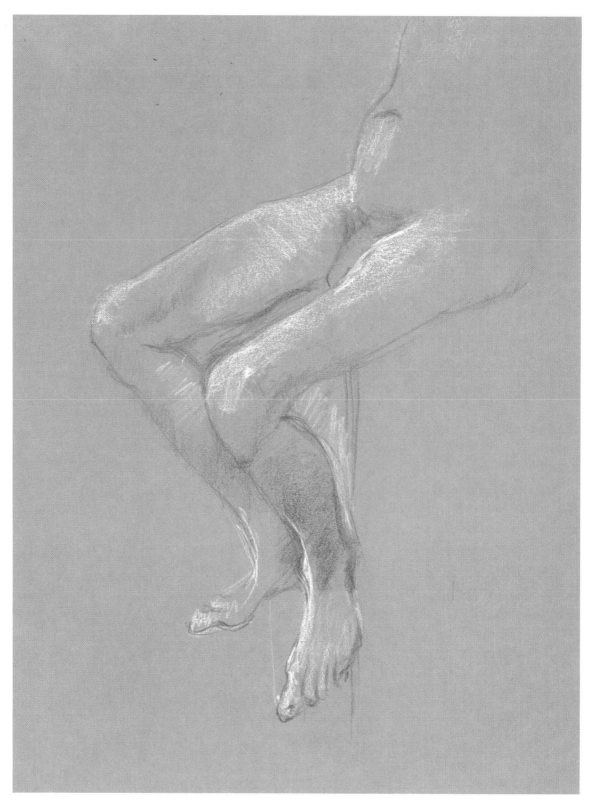

Opposite Form not only applies to the solidity of flesh and bone but also to the invisible plane across the thighs of a seated model. (*Pencil highlighted with chalk 11 x 8 in/ 28 x 20 cm*)

Imagine sheets of transparent polythene or cling film were used to wrap and draw together various facets of the figure. This will prompt you to see your subject at first in simple, large blocks and masses in space rather than as a series of disconnected details.

But the structure of the human figure contains even more: it has roundness and density, firmness and softness, rigidity and flexibility,

Above Sensitive observation of the textural variety increases the likelihood of producing a convincing drawing. (*Sanguine pencil 5 x 8 in/13 x 20 cm*)

roughness and smoothness. Look for all these tactile variations as you place your pencil, chalk or brush upon the paper. Imagine you are placing it directly on to the figure in front of you and try to feel through the marks you make the quality of the bone, muscle, skin or hair: a delicate touch for round soft areas, firm strokes where the bones show on the surface, wiry or silken texture for the hair. Be continually conscious of all this subtle tactility.

When you try to describe a contour, be aware that it is only seen as a contour because the form itself is turning away from you in perspective.

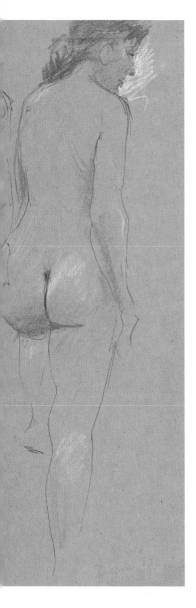

If you were to move your viewpoint a few inches either way, the contours would change. The quality of the line you draw will convey the extent to which you are conscious of this.

Also use the technique of 'reading across' to help to understand how the form exists in three-dimensional space. This term describes the action of visually relating pairs of features across the figure: being conscious of the position of the left shoulder, for example, as you draw the right one, or the right hip as you draw the left, one cheekbone with the other, and so forth. This applies even when you can see only one side clearly; it is the structural analysis of the hidden part that will help you render the visible part in context. Eventually you will begin to find that your drawing appears to exist within three-dimensional space and is no longer looking like a flat cut-out.

Weight

Gravitational pull dictates the weight of all solid matter. In human beings this is evident both when they are active and when they are passive. It is the fundamental influence on the shape and quality of the stance in a life pose. It affects how the shoulders drop and how the arms hang. Gravity also affects the surface anatomy. In a seated pose, for example, look for those clues like the spreading of the buttocks and the folding of the abdomen. See how the weight of a model's hand resting on the thighs indents into the flesh. In a reclining pose observe how the torso and hips become flattened underneath.

The weight is all important in the analysis and understanding of the posture. As you study the figure, ask yourself why certain areas of the body appear to alter whenever the pose changes: what happens when the model's arms are raised, or when the model kneels? Think of the multitude of ways the body weight is distributed and influences the stance, and watch for these as you start each new drawing. Without going into too much detail, you should establish the surface on which the model is seated or reclined in order to give contrast to the form and a base for the pose.

Above Contours are continuations of the form seen in perspective. (*Pencil, ink and chalk 18 x 6 in/ 46 x 15 cm*)

Opposite Bodyweight is evident in features such as the spreading of the buttocks of a seated model. (*Coloured pencils 16 x 12 in/ 40.5 x 30.5 cm*)

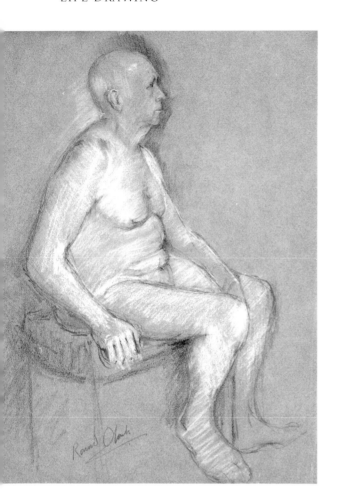

Basic Anatomy

Although it is not necessary to have a clinical understanding of anatomy to enjoy life drawing, a small vocabulary of the general anatomical terms and some knowledge of how the main bones and muscles function inevitably increases one's appreciation of what is happening in a pose.

The skeleton of the human body is by any definition a wonderful piece of engineering. Although everybody possesses the same number of bones, they can greatly differ in size and shape, thus determining much of what we call the build of a person. For the purposes of defining the various terms, the skeleton can be roughly divided into five parts: the spinal column and ribcage, the pelvic area, the upper and lower limbs and the skull.

Weight is also apparent in the abdomenal folds in a seated posture, and the squashing together of the leg muscles in a kneeling posture. (*Pastels: left 16 x 12 in/40.5 x 30.5 cm; right 16 x 11 in/40.5 x 28 cm*)

The spine, which has four curves seen from the sides, is composed of 26 vertebrae (33 in children) which are single units connected together around the spinal cord. From the skull down they are made up from 7 cervical vertebrae in the neck, 12 thoracic vertebrae to which the ribs are attached, 5 lumbar vertebrae in the small of the back, the sacrum made of 5 vertebrae fused together in adulthood and, finally, 4 vertebrae united to form the coccyx, the vestigial signs of a tail. The spine is the central core around and upon which everything else functions and depends. It is the main support for the skull, the ribcage, and, through the pelvis, the lower limbs. It is capable of bending forwards, backwards and sideways, as well as twisting. When drawing a figure, you should always be aware of the direction of the spinal column.

The ribcage is made up of 12 pairs of ribs, each pair growing from a single vertebra and curving round to the front of the chest where, apart from the lower two pairs, they are joined together at the sternum, or breast bone. The lower two pairs are free at the front and thus called 'floating' ribs. The ribcage envelops and protects the vital organs of the upper body, the heart, lungs and liver.

The pelvis is also joined to the spine but at the place where the five sacrum vertebrae are fused together. It is shaped roughly like a hollow dish with wings. It not only acts as a bridge between the spine and the upper leg bones but also as a protective basket supporting the reproductive organs in females and the final stages of the digestive system in both sexes. The crests of the upper part of the pelvis, known as the ilium, can be clearly seen and felt just below the waist. The very lowest projections beneath the seat are called the ischium which are fused in adulthood to the low frontal crescent called the pubis.

What we call the hip-bone, another fairly prominent projection, is technically known as the greater trochanter, a bony outer extension at the head of the femur (thigh bone), the longest bone in the body. The femur is inserted into the pelvis by a ball-and-socket joint of tremendous strength, and it is this 'ball' which is replaced in operations to repair arthritic damage to hips.

The lower leg consists of two main bones, the tibia and the fibula. The tibia, or shin bone, is the supporting bone and is appropriately large and thick. It is clearly visible in anybody's leg. The upper end forms part of the knee joint together with the lower end of the femur, and fronting the joint between these is the patella or kneecap. The fibula is a thinner bone, slightly shorter than the tibia and attached to it both near the top and at the ankle, where it helps to rotate the foot. The foot is made up of a number of smaller bones: calcaneum (heel bone); tarsals that articulate the foot; metatarsals running down to the toes; and phalanges (toe bones).

The arms are attached to the upper body at the shoulder joint where

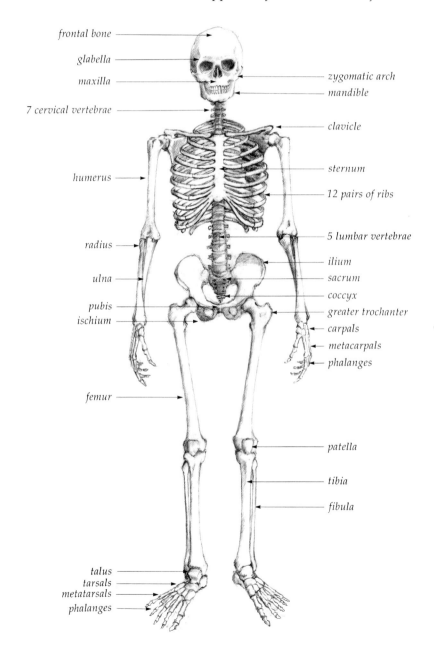

frontal bone
glabella
maxilla
7 cervical vertebrae
humerus
radius
ulna
pubis
ischium
femur
talus
tarsals
metatarsals
phalanges

zygomatic arch
mandible
clavicle
sternum
12 pairs of ribs
5 lumbar vertebrae
ilium
sacrum
coccyx
greater trochanter
carpals
metacarpals
phalanges
patella
tibia
fibula

the top end of the humerus (the long bone in the upper arm) is inserted into the cavity of a winged projection in the scapula (shoulder blade), a triangular blade of bone which slides across the back of the ribcage. Also at the junction point is one end of the clavicle (collar bone), a long thin curving bone which is joined by ligaments at its other end to the top of the sternum. The clavicle is involved in many of the movements of the

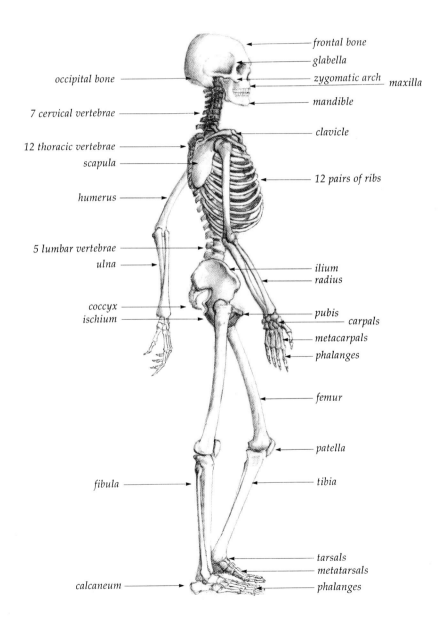

frontal bone
glabella
occipital bone
zygomatic arch   *maxilla*
mandible
7 cervical vertebrae
clavicle
12 thoracic vertebrae
scapula
12 pairs of ribs
humerus
5 lumbar vertebrae
ulna
ilium
radius
coccyx
ischium
pubis
carpals
metacarpals
phalanges
femur
patella
fibula
tibia
tarsals
metatarsals
calcaneum
phalanges

upper arms and shoulders, and is particularly noticeable with regard to counterbalancing pelvic tilt.

The forearm comprises two longish bones, the ulna and the radius. The ulna, one end of which forms part of the elbow joint, represents the strength of the forearm and elbow, while the slightly thinner radius performs the rotating action of the wrist. The hand bones are very similar in type to the foot bones and consist of the eight carpal bones of the wrist, the metacarpal bones in the back of the hand, and the phalanges (the jointed bones of the fingers).

Finally the skull which, for purposes of isolating those areas most distinctive for drawing purposes, can be divided into two main parts: the cranium which protects the brain, and the facial bones. Of the cranium, the dome of the forehead is called the frontal bone, and the lower back of the head is known as the occipital bone. The most significant facial areas are the glabella (ridge of the eyebrow), the zygomatic arch (cheekbone), the maxilla (upper jaw) and mandible (lower jaw).

The musculature system is the cladding of our structure. It is only necessary here to discuss it in the broadest terms and in connection with how the surface appearance affects the shapes we see when drawing.

Different muscles perform different duties. Some manipulate the hinges of a joint while others hold various parts of the body erect, thus preventing us from literally falling apart. Whenever you look closely at a pose, try to determine which muscles are flexed – those taking the strain or weight of the posture – and which remain relaxed. Since the muscle distribution is symmetrical – whatever appears on one side of the body has its mirror image on the other – you can often compare a contracted muscle with its relaxed partner on the other side. The process known as 'reading across' is useful here (*see* Form and Texture, page 30).

To help with your perception of the physical tensions, it is useful to know what the main surface muscles are called and what they do. Generally speaking, muscles are attached at both ends to bone. It may be to different parts of the same bone or to two associated bones as in the case of the biceps in the upper arm. Here the muscle attaches to the humerus in the upper arm and the ulna in the forearm, thus becoming the operating force for the elbow joint. Flexing the biceps shortens or contracts it so that the joint closes. In contrast the triceps, attached to the back of the humerus, contracts when the arm is pushed out straight,

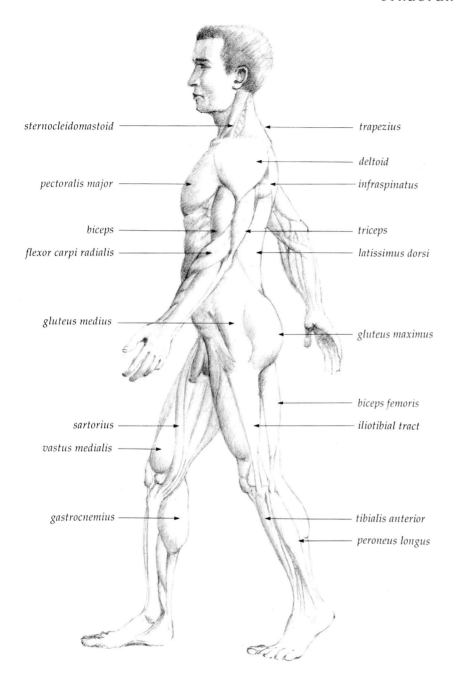

sternocleidomastoid

pectoralis major

biceps

flexor carpi radialis

gluteus medius

sartorius

vastus medialis

gastrocnemius

trapezius

deltoid

infraspinatus

triceps

latissimus dorsi

gluteus maximus

biceps femoris

iliotibial tract

tibialis anterior

peroneus longus

whereas the main muscle of the forearm, the flexor carpi radialis, will tense as you rotate the wrist. Try these movements for yourself and feel how these muscles alternately tighten and relax as you bend, straighten and rotate your arm. Then try flexing and relaxing other parts of your body to see which muscles contract.

The neck has two main muscles, of which the outer one is the stern-

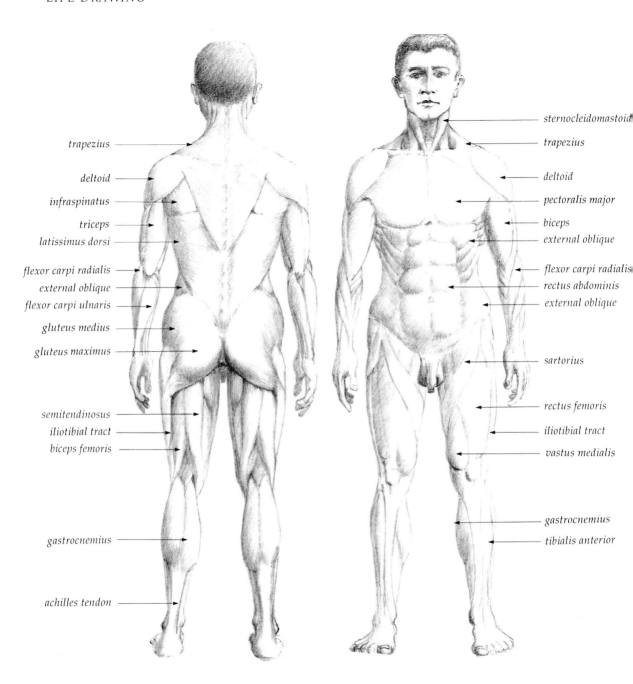

trapezius

deltoid

infraspinatus

triceps

latissimus dorsi

flexor carpi radialis

external oblique

flexor carpi ulnaris

gluteus medius

gluteus maximus

semitendinosus

iliotibial tract

biceps femoris

gastrocnemius

achilles tendon

sternocleidomastoid

trapezius

deltoid

pectoralis major

biceps

external oblique

flexor carpi radialis

rectus abdominis

external oblique

sartorius

rectus femoris

iliotibial tract

vastus medialis

gastrocnemius

tibialis anterior

ocleidomastoid muscle which helps to move the head. At the back of the upper torso are two large triangular muscles, called trapezius, running from the neck down either side of the spinal column to help to keep the neck and head upright. At the sides of the torso lower down are the latissimus dorsi, large sheets of muscle which turn the trunk. Covering the outside of the shoulders are the deltoid muscles whose function is to raise the arms and are so named because they are triangular-shaped like the Greek letter delta. Covering the chest are the pectoralis major, large muscles that flex when you squeeze your arms together. The mammalian glands (breasts) on a woman are superimposed on the pectoralis major.

The group of ridged muscles in the front of the abdomen, called the rectus abdominis, allow the trunk to bend forward. At each side of these are the external oblique muscles which work to draw the side of the ribcage and the pelvis together.

Moving further down the body, the large muscles of the buttocks are called gluteus maximus while those running over the hips are the gluteus medius. The main muscle at the back of the thigh operating the knee joint is the biceps femoris; that running down the full length of the outside of the thigh, giving power to the lower leg, is the iliotibial tract; the one transversing from the top front of the thigh down to the lower inside, clearly seen flexing when the leg is lifted, is the sartorius; and that at the front of the thigh is the rectus femoris. At the front of the lower leg is the tibialis anterior which helps to raise the foot and the muscle in the calf, giving strength to the leg, is called the gastrocnemius.

This is by no means an exhaustive description of human anatomy and does not include any specific references to the female body, but it should help in identifying and understanding many of the tensions and forces seen in any nude pose.

Perspective and Foreshortening

The study of perspective may not seem to be altogether relevant in the life class. Its direct application is not perhaps so immediately obvious as it might be to, say, the student of landscape or pictorial composition. However, once the draughtsman has begun to examine the pose closely, it should become clear that quite a number of the problems confronted relate to those of perspective. Whatever the viewpoint from which your drawing is made, much of the model will be seen to be above or below your own eye level (the horizon line) – probably both.

Take, for example, the thighs of a model seated on a chair or stool. Unless these are seen precisely from sideways-on at eye level, there will be some element of perspective, varying by degrees depending on how

much of the sides can be seen. Invariably the legs will appear below eye level so the thighs will seem to slope up as they recede from you. If they are seen acutely from the front, with little or no sides visible, we describe them as being foreshortened. Any part of the body seen along its length is similarly referred to as being foreshortened.

A reclining pose seen from one end creates particular problems of perspective with regard to the relative size of the head or the feet to the rest of the body. It is essential to take visual measurements of their relationships because their normal ratio cannot be presumed and in such circumstances may be surprising. When drawing a standing figure where the head is well above your own eye level, be aware of the apparent slope of the eyes, the mouth, the shoulders and the ribcage. Notice also below your eye level how the foot furthest away from you appears to be above the one closer to you. These are all evidence of perspective, a greater understanding of which will be appreciated by paying particular attention to 'reading across' at as many points and pairs of features as you possibly can. (*See* Form and Texture, page 30.)

The Viewpoint

Unless the pose has been set for a very short duration, it is worth taking some time before settling on a viewpoint. Consider the composition, distance, perspective, lighting, background and anything else which may influence your involvement. There is little benefit in accepting the viewpoint from the position where you happen to be if there is a better angle elsewhere. You might also try drawing the same pose from two or three different angles, combining them for comparison on the same sheet. Attempt to keep them all in proportion if you can and execute each one within approximately the same length of time.

If the conditions allow it, be prepared to try drawing from either a high viewpoint – on top of a table or some ladder steps, for instance – or from a very low angle close to floor level. The sensation of looking at the figure from these unfamiliar angles can prompt you to see it fresh, as though for the first time, which is the frame of mind we should always be trying to induce.

The foreshortening from above will test your powers of direct obser-

Above Features above eye level appear to slope down and those below slope up. (*Black and white pastels 20 x 9 in/51 x 23 cm*)

Opposite A seated nude showing foreshortening of the thigh and forearm. (*Sanguine wash 14 x 10 in/ 35.5 x 25.5 cm*)

41

vation because you probably will not be able to rely on what you already know, or what you have done before, but only on what you can see here and now. For example, notice from above how the head appears to be enlarged in comparison to the remainder of the figure, possibly much larger than you can ever have imagined it might be. By contrast the dramatic effect of a low eye level presents many other challenges. It is essential that you carry on with checking the measurements when drawing from these unusual viewpoints because relative proportions can appear so different from what are considered to be the norm.

Some of the Italian and Flemish painters of the seventeenth and eighteenth centuries give perfect examples of how sensational figures can appear when depicted from unusual viewpoints. Artists such as Rubens and Tiepolo produced highly dramatic representations in their work where angels, cherubs or other celestial beings (all in human form) are shown floating in, or ascending to heaven. The viewpoint was often that of the earthbound so the figures were invariably depicted in unfamiliar positions. Similarly, earlier masters like Michelangelo produced drawings

The more unusual the viewpoint, the more important it is to keep measuring and comparing different features. (*Sepia wash highlighted with white chalk 14 x 20 in/ 35.5 x 51 cm*)

A drawing made from a low viewpoint clearly demonstrated by the perspective of the window behind the model.
(Black and white pastels on grey paper 19 x 14 in/ 48 x 35.5 cm)

and paintings of the human figure at constricted or abnormal angles to fit within architectural recesses such as an apsis or cupola. Although drawing from an unusual viewpoint may cause you to experience some temporary discomfort, the compensations are well worthwhile.

Part 2
MEDIA AND TECHNIQUE

'A man paints with his brain and not with his hands.' – Michelangelo

Some readers may feel that a book on life drawing should have begun with an introduction to various drawing implements followed by lots of useful tips on technique. But it is my belief that the art is in the seeing, much more than in the rendering of any particular medium. It is not through the sharpness of your pencil, the quality of your paper or in the practising of shading that improvements in your drawing will be achieved, but only by developing a greater awareness of what is happening in front of your eyes.

However, drawings do have to be set down on some base material or support and marks need to be made with one implement or another, so it is as well to learn what kind of results can be obtained using different types of instrument and media. Furthermore, a change of medium can sometimes help to stimulate flagging powers of observation. The medium you choose will, to a lesser or greater degree, dictate the style of drawing you do and prompt you to observe the model accordingly. With this in mind, consider carrying out several drawings from the same viewpoint using a variety of implements: pencil, charcoal, pastels, ink and wash. Observe how the change of medium alters your response to what you see. As you try each in turn, you will appreciate that different materials are more sympathetic to certain kinds of interpretation. For example, there is no point in attempting a fine detailed drawing with a stick of charcoal, it just cannot be manipulated precisely enough. Conversely, pen and ink is not ideal for the production of large-scale dynamic drawings with dramatic tonal contrasts. But always beware the seduction of technique for its own sake.

A sepia pen and wash study on a lightly tinted paper – a classic medium for life drawing.
(15 x 11 in/38 x 28 cm)

45

Pencil and Graphite Stick

Of all the media available for drawing, graphite or 'lead' pencil is the one by far the most frequently used in life studies. This is partly due to its ease of access and its portability, but also because of a long tradition dating back to the early nineteenth century when the range of graphite shades was first introduced, allowing the artist to render instant gradations of line and tone. A similar medium called silver-point was used prior to this, particularly effectively in the fifteenth and sixteenth centuries in both Italy and northern Europe by masters such as Leonardo da Vinci and Albrecht Dürer. Today, most students begin their drawing studies with the pencil and there are one or two tips worth considering.

As with any craft or skill, the tools and equipment employed should be kept in good condition. A finely sharpened pencil will not of itself produce a fine drawing, but it will be one less thing to worry about, one less obstacle to come between you and your subject. Struggling with a blunt, worn out pencil could soon reduce your concentration and ultimately frustration may spoil your enjoyment. A pencil with a long sharp

The point of a pencil can be used to describe the contours of a figure while its edge can be used for shading the form. (*Left 5 x 4 in/13 x 10 cm; right 13 x 10 in/33 x 25.5 cm*)

The form and texture of
the figure can be explored
by building a gradation of
tones with the pencil.
(11 x 9 in/28 x 23 cm)

point is more adaptable for the purpose than one with a short sharp
point because it can be held either in the writer's grip for linear marks, or
as if holding a very slender torch allowing the side of the graphite cone
to be used for tonal gradation. Practise the technique of building graduated shades from a ghostly faintness to an almost solid depth of tone.
Rehearse until the use of the pencil becomes second nature – an extension of your own hand. The less you need to think about the medium,
the more effort and concentration you can spend on developing your
powers of perception.

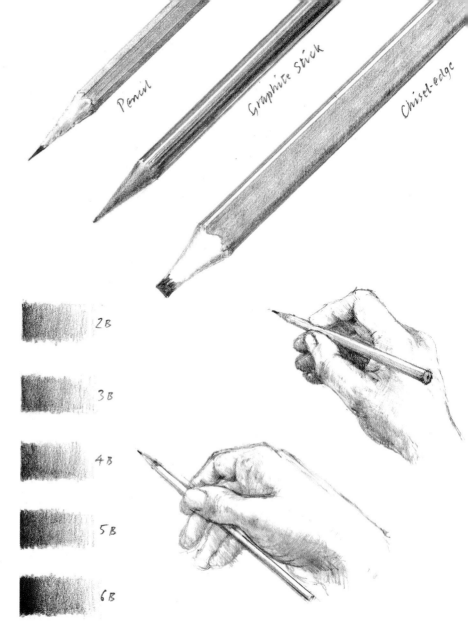

Pencils and graphite sticks are manufactured in a wide range of tonal grades. Either the pen-holder grip or the 'torch' grip can be used depending on the marks to be made.

Pencils are manufactured in a wide variety of grades from very hard to very soft: from 9H, which is as hard and fine as a needle, through to 9B, which is very thick and black. For life drawing I find the most useful are probably those from 2B to 6B inclusive, although each individual draughtsman may have other preferences.

Graphite sticks are pencil-sized implements made from the same material as the so-called 'lead' pencil but without the wooden casing. Protected by a plastic sheath, solid graphite sticks are a good deal more expensive than ordinary pencils but, while their quality of softness is classified on the same scale as pencils, and sharpened in much the same way, they last very much longer and have the added advantage that, when the sharpened cone is used on its side, it makes a broader single mark than the equivalent grade of pencil. This allows the blocking-in of tone to be that much more rapid.

Pencils can be used on almost any kind and quality of paper but generally cartridge is considered to be the best. Always begin your drawing with the express intention of not using an eraser. You will find this will induce you to progress prudently, building layer upon layer, making corrections but allowing the previous, more lightly rendered marks to remain. If you start off by using a B or 2B, you will have the darker shades left in reserve for later adjustments. Feel your way slowly and do not settle on absolutes too early. Treated with understanding, respect and a certain amount of finesse, a pencil can respond almost like a magic wand.

Charcoal

Charcoal – sticks of charred wood, invariably willow – is thought to have been used as a drawing medium in ancient Greece although evidence of extant drawings only goes back as far as the early sixteenth century. Boxed collections of sticks can be purchased today in three grades: thin, medium and thick. Unlike pencils, all possess the same blackness of application although there is a brown pigment called bistre which is also made from charred wood.

Many students using charcoal for the first time try to make it perform like a pencil by using the tip to draw in the contours. This is a mistake because not only is it incapable of the precision of a pencil but its real potential is being ignored. Charcoal is the ideal medium for executing large, full-blooded drawings with vigour and directness, and it can be beneficial in releasing you from a lot of the inhibitions that might be caused by the production of a series of smaller, tighter studies in pencil. As well as drawing with the tip, try breaking a stick in half and using the side for large sweeping areas of shadow or background. Think large! Set your parameters as discussed in Planning and Building, page 15, then without a lot of measuring and plotting, lay in the basic stance swiftly and boldly. Sweep in the curvature of the spine and the angles of the limbs and head. If the background is generally darker in tone than the subject, sketch this in with the side of the stick, leaving the figure white. And, where they appear, use the negative shapes to bring out the silhouette of the arms and legs. Modelling of the form can then proceed by employing a combination of charcoal stick and rubbing with the fingers.

The nature of its make-up dictates that the marks made by charcoal are very easily smudged which, to the artist, is both an asset and a drawback. Its unique advantage rests in the fact that by rubbing with the fingers, or with a tightly rolled cone of paper called a stump, it is the perfect medium for manipulating and reworking form and texture. Corrections to unwanted lines and repositioning shadows are far easier than with almost any other drawing medium and can be made indefinitely. There is no amount of rough application that cannot be adjusted or repaired as

Opposite Charcoal is the ideal medium for swiftly and boldly sketching in the nude figure against a darkened background. *(19 x 16 in/48 x 40.5 cm)*

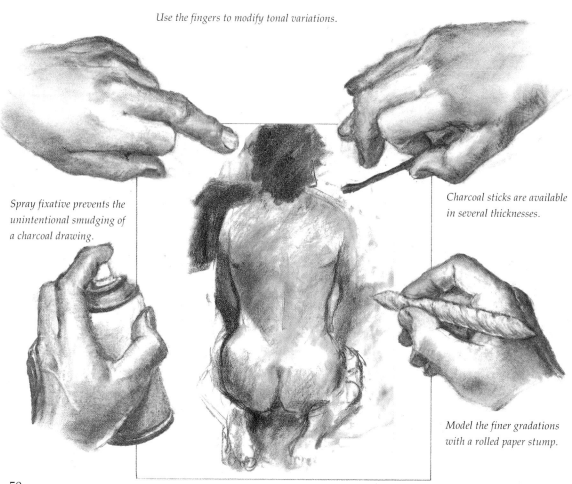

Use the fingers to modify tonal variations.

Spray fixative prevents the unintentional smudging of a charcoal drawing.

Charcoal sticks are available in several thicknesses.

Model the finer gradations with a rolled paper stump.

the drawing develops. Charcoal is the most forgiving of drawing materials. Whole areas can be removed or modified with a kneaded 'putty' rubber which, in an ideal world, should only be employed as an additional drawing instrument rather than as a mere eraser. When used on a tinted paper, charcoal can very effectively be combined with white or light grey pastels to define the highlights.

To prevent accidental smudging – the main disadvantage of the medium – a mahlstick (a light stick with a padded leather ball at one end) can be employed during the final stages to help to keep your drawing hand clear of your work. Alternatively, it may be advisable to use a fixative (spray varnish) at intervals throughout the drawing session. This allows you, after a minute or so, to continue working on top of the drawing but no longer to erase any work that has been fixed. Generally, one has to be that extra bit more careful not to damage the drawing when resting a hand on the paper. Except when deliberately rubbing with the fingers, it may be best to work at arm's length and allow only the charcoal stick to touch the surface. Where appropriate it is sometimes worth trying to draw with the other hand to avoid any smudging. (The symmetrical subject on page 101 was drawn to some extent with charcoal sticks simultaneously in both hands.) On completing your drawing, you must remember to spray it immediately with fixative because the act of rolling it up to carry it home before it has been fixed could badly spoil much of your efforts.

Opposite above When pastels are used on a white or cream paper, the background tones should be established early on to bring the figure into relief. *(16 x 11 in/40.5 x 28 cm)*

Opposite below On a mid-toned paper, this male nude was drawn in black and white pastels only, allowing the coloured paper to serve as the mid tones. *(19 x 14 in/ 48 x 35.5 cm)*

Soft Pastels

Unlike oil pastels, which are like rather greasy crayons, soft pastels are more like very finely made chalks. They can be of different densities, different thicknesses, either round- or square-ended and come in a wide range of colours (*see* Coloured Pastels, page 62). Only those used for monochrome or sanguine drawings are considered here.

Between black and white there are many shades of grey and with these, or a selection of them, a worthwhile exercise is to try drawing only in light and shade, avoiding any temptation to adopt a linear technique. Imagine instead you are bathing the form in light rather than merely applying pigment to paper. This is best done working on a toned paper

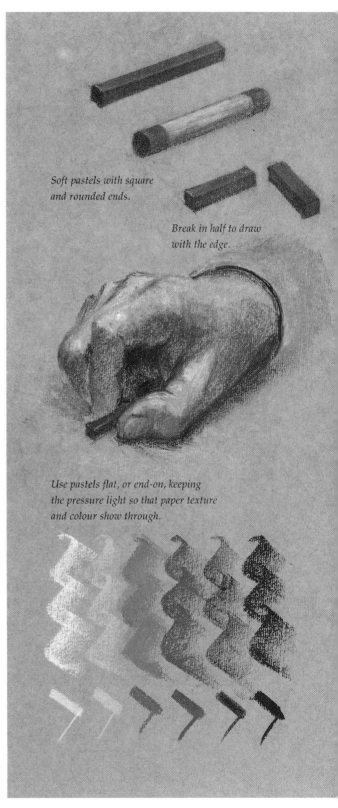

Soft pastels with square
and rounded ends.

Break in half to draw
with the edge.

Use pastels flat, or end-on, keeping
the pressure light so that paper texture
and colour show through.

but it can also be adapted to white grounds as well. When choosing a tinted paper, select one which is fairly neutral in colour (warm grey or mid brown, for example), medium in tone – not too light and not too dark – and one with a slight texture or 'tooth' such as Ingres, Canford or Canson. A cheaper sugar paper is all right except it will lose its colour in the course of time.

As you start your drawing, first decide where the brightest highlight is and show this with the lightest tone of pastel you have. (If you are drawing on a white ground, this area will be left blank.) Secondly, decide where and what is the deepest shadow: it may be in the hair, or underneath the figure, or in the background. Wherever it is, it should be shown in the darkest next to black of the pigments you have (black will be needed ultimately for emphasizing points of detail). All other tones you subsequently see and apply will belong somewhere on a scale between these two extremes and the tone of each area you depict must be selected relative to this scale of values. Finally, when you want to delineate the sharper shadow lines – where two areas of flesh meet

In a pastel drawing, it is worth attempting to 'bathe' the form with light instead of trying to follow the contour. (*8 x 11 in/ 20 x 28 cm*)

tightly, such as under the armpits or between the buttocks – you can make use of a sharpened black pastel or a pastel pencil.

Try to apply the shades in wide, definite strokes, using either the flattened end or the side of the chalk broken in half, following the planes of the form rather than smudging the gradations together. Keep the pressure light so that the chalk adheres only to the raised surface of the textured paper, allowing some of the background to show through. You can always build up to a more solid application later if necessary.

It often helps to see different tonal values by half closing your eyes and squinting at the subject so that you see the whole figure only in terms of tones without the distraction of any detail. Although this is not a technique that is immediately attainable and one that requires both patience and practice, it is well worth persevering with. In a drawing of this kind, remember the tones in the background are equally important as those within the subject itself. The tint of the paper can often be used to serve as areas of mid tone in the figure. One exercise is to restrict your pastels simply to black and white on a grey ground.

Sanguine is a French term meaning blood-coloured and is used to describe drawings prepared in ruddy-brown hues made from iron oxide. There is a tradition of drawing in this red chalk that goes back as far as sixteenth-century Renaissance Italy when master draughtsmen such as Raphael and Andrea del Sarto were at the height of their powers. Its warm subtle qualities are extremely sympathetic for life studies, particularly when applied on cream-coloured paper.

Pen, Ink and Wash

There is no single 'correct' method of drawing with pen and ink. It is a medium that can be used in a variety of styles as any cursory study of the Old Masters will demonstrate. You may need to experiment with a number until you find a pen and a style which are comfortable for you – not simply because the medium affords a superficially attractive result, but because once it becomes familiar to you, it will not get in the way between you and your subject. Nothing is more frustrating than attempting to draw with an implement that stubbornly refuses to make free and easy marks on the paper.

A dip pen is the most flexible type since it can be fitted with a variety of nibs. Some nibs are fairly stiff and resistant while others are quite springy and yielding. Before you start, unless you are using a brand new nib, it is important to clean off all the old dried-up ink by scraping gently all over it with a penknife until the surface shines. This will greatly ease the flow of ink. Then once the nib is fully charged with ink, practise gently increasing the pressure as you draw and you will see just how much variation of line thickness can be achieved. A variable thickness of line is more conducive in defining the curving contours of the form, and while this may take a little practice, it will eventually become second nature. To render an even finer line, try drawing with the back of the nib.

Fountain and cartridge pens are very convenient for quick sketches because they do not need to be dipped into the ink but, although there is a selection of thicknesses of nib, they lack the flexibility of dip pens. Ink cartridges are available, among other colours, in black, sepia or brown, which are those most agreeable for life studies.

Ball-points, and to some extent technical pens, are also convenient but they have the disadvantage of producing a monoline mark lacking any variety of thickness, which can be a handicap when trying to describe subtleties of contour and form. However, they are almost totally dependable whereas fountain pens can sometimes dry up at crucial moments.

Cross-hatching is a traditional method of shading, not only with pen and ink but also with etching and engraving tools, by using regular strokes overlapping in two different directions. Sensitively applied, as it was by great masters like Michelangelo and Dürer, it is a time-honoured technique which can be used to describe complicated and intricate muscle formation. However, it has inherent dangers of appearing rather mechanical and mannered when used in a purely artificial way. It is probably at its best where the overlapping lines create a tiny diamond-shaped texture rather than a square-shaped one. What is important is that the lines follow the direction of the form – that is, around a limb in the direction of the perspective.

Some inks are waterproof and some are water-soluble. India ink will give a very solid black line which some draughtsmen may find too harsh and unsubtle for life drawing. Water-soluble inks or concentrated watercolours are preferable, particularly those in the sepia, brown or sanguine

A drawing in sepia wash overdrawn with pen and brown ink. (*13 x 10 in/ 33 x 25.5 cm*)

colours, because they are not only sympathetic in colour but can also be diluted with water to varying degrees of tonal density. This is ideal when combining pen with wash – the term used when referring to diluted watercolour or ink applied with a medium or large watercolour brush.

This method of application requires having a suitable container or mixing tray with two or three compartments in which diluted ink in varying strengths can be mixed. Using plenty of clean water, brush in the

Opposite Two pen drawings rapidly produced, one overlaid with a light wash. (*Left 14 x 5 in/35.5 x 13 cm; right 15 x 5 in/38 x 13 cm*)

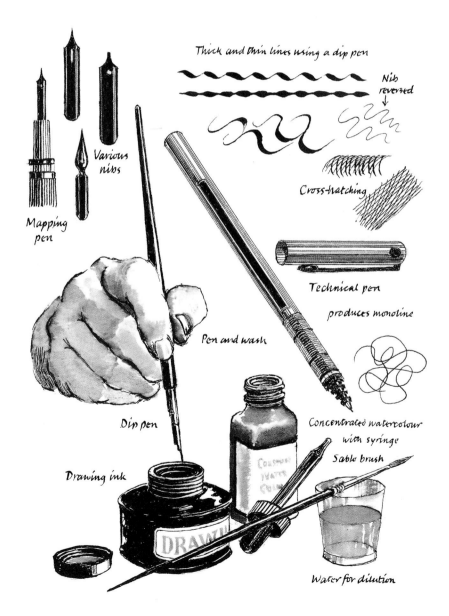

Thick and thin lines using a dip pen

Nib reversed

Cross-hatching

Various nibs

Mapping pen

Technical pen

produces monoline

Pen and wash

Concentrated watercolour with syringe

Dip pen

Sable brush

Drawing ink

Water for dilution

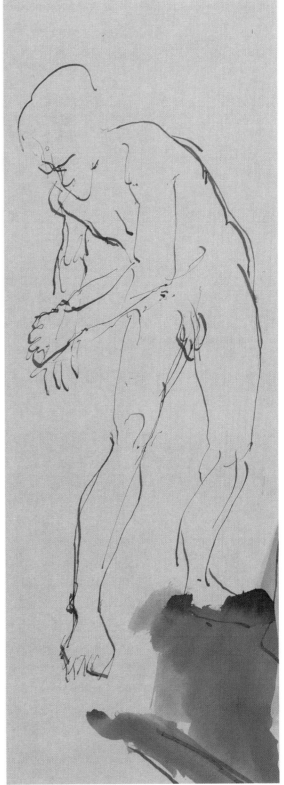

shadow washes of your drawing. Then, using the brush to fill your pen-nib with a slightly darker shade of ink (do not dip the pen in the conventional way), draw into those washed-in areas. Alternatively, the pen work can precede the wash. Try both methods and carry on using them alternately, first on a dry ground and then on a dampened one. Ordinary cartridge paper can be used, but if the surface is to be subjected to a good deal of soaking, a specialist watercolour paper stretched on to a board is better.

Mixed Media

Purist rules condemning the use of more than one medium in the same work as 'contamination', reduce the art of drawing to that of a craft where long-established techniques and procedures are inviolable. Drawing, in my opinion, should not be regarded in that way since the freedom to investigate and experiment is fundamental.

There might be one of several reasons for mixing two or more kinds of media in a life study. It may occur either by planned design or by events arising as the drawing develops. Deliberately combining materials implies previous experience gained either fortuitously, or through experimentation, or by witness of another's work. Sometimes a particular rendering may not be expressing exactly what you see before you. You may begin to perceive larger and bolder relationships not initially apparent but which are beyond the scope of the medium you have chosen. Conversely, a material like chalk or charcoal might be found to be too imprecise for the depiction of fine, delicate detail. Although it may be tempting simply to abandon the drawing and begin again, when so much effort has already gone into it why not try working on top with another more sympathetic technique? Another reason may be because the medium you have chosen is becoming too confused with many correction lines. In this case overdrawing with another, more incisive medium could be the way forward.

Provided there are no physical properties to prevent their combining, any two or more materials can be used together. You will find that charcoal and pastel will not go too easily over graphite because the graphite leaves a shiny surface to which the softer materials will not adhere. But

A quick study begun in pencil, continued with brown wash and finished in pen and ink.
(*12 x 8 in/30.5 x 20 cm*)

A drawing in pen and wash highlighted with white pastel on tinted paper. (*15 x 15 in/ 38 x 38 cm*)

graphite will take perfectly satisfactorily on top of the other two. Pastels combine very well with pen and wash and are particularly useful for the adding of highlights. Watercolours that are well worked occasionally become too darkened in places where highlights should appear and no amount of 'washing out' successfully brings back the lightness required. In these circumstances try either a little body colour (gouache or tube watercolour), or pastels. Try experimenting with a number of different associations of pencil, chalk, charcoal, ink and paints.

Colour

The application of colour takes us into that obscure area where drawing meets painting. Apart from oil and some acrylic painting I can see no clear distinction between the two; a watercolour study can equally be termed a painting or a drawing. Colour is not something that can be added to monochrome drawings as an afterthought because it needs to be planned from the beginning. Looking for tonal values in the nude model is different from looking for colour values, although there is some common ground where colour is influenced by light and shade.

Coloured Pastels

Pastels have been continuously and widely employed for life studies in colour ever since Degas revived their use during the second half of the nineteenth century, after which the other Impressionists were similarly impelled to recognize the inherent qualities in them for recording subtleties of colour and light.

Their delicate texture and their ease of both application and portability offer advantages that are lacking in other colour media such as oil paint, acrylics or watercolour. There are some drawbacks, however. What is easily applied is also easily smudged and damaged. The sticks crumble and break when too much pressure is used, or if they are accidentally dropped. And, although the range of colours is infinitely subtle in the lighter shades, it is less so in the darker. In spite of these minor difficulties, however, they are incomparable for bringing out the soft, rich skin tones of the nude figure.

In my view pastels are at their best when used on a tinted paper, neutral in colour such as grey, ochre or brown, with a slight texture or 'tooth' to allow the pigment to adhere easily. Although they can also be used on a white paper such as cartridge, the disadvantage is that much of the background around the figure first needs to be filled in before the light reflected from the form can be fully and convincingly captured.

For life studies, select a range of harmonizing tints restricting them to no more than, say, 15–18. Unless the model is posed against strongly coloured drapes or there are colourful props involved, half a dozen or so

Pastels are incomparable for bringing out the soft, rich skin tones of the nude figure. (*16 x 12 in/ 40.5 x 30.5 cm*)

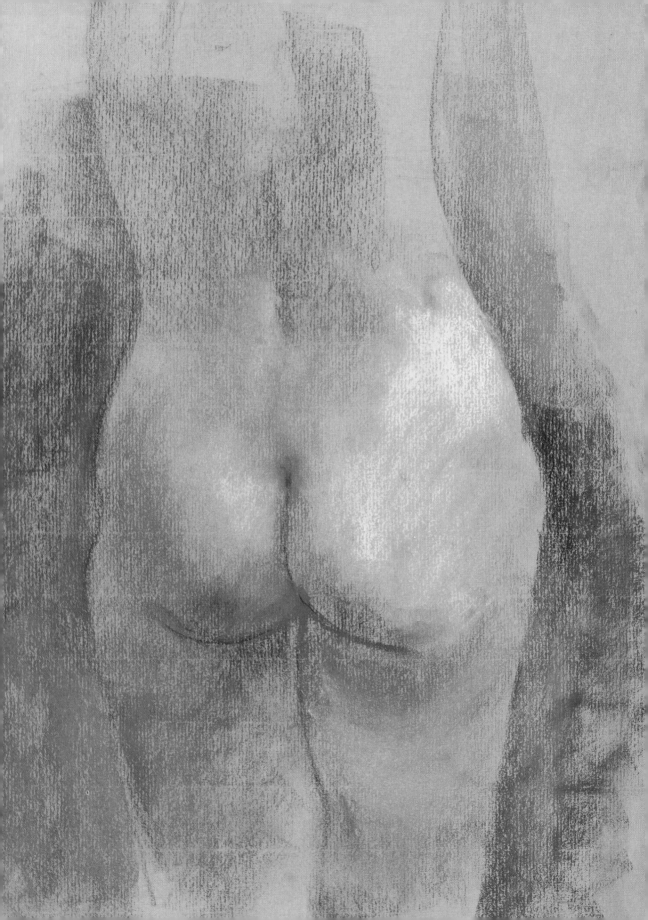

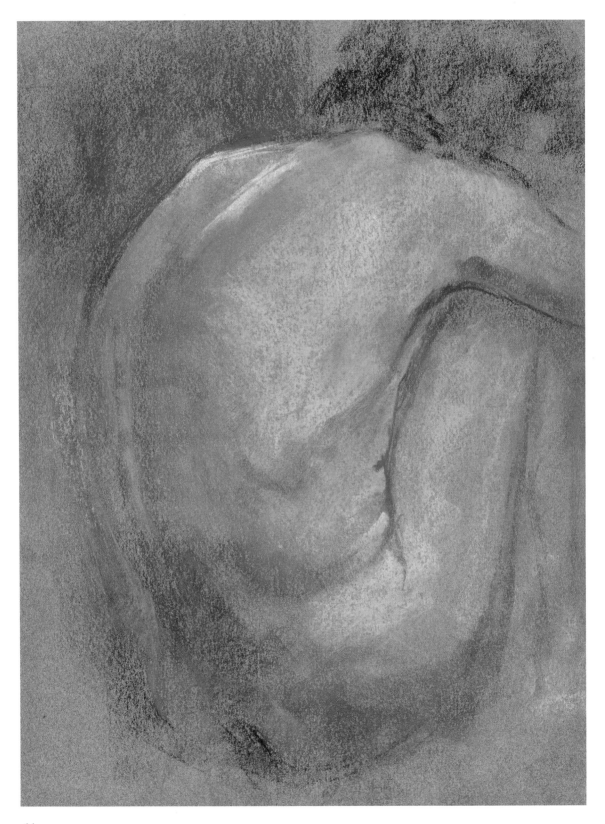

A male torso drawn with the harmonious, but limited, range of pastels shown above. *(12 x 9 in/ 30.5 x 23 cm)*

sticks from the cream/pink/red/brown range could be enough, together with perhaps two or three greys, greens and blues for the cooler shadow areas. And you will almost certainly need black for the deepest shadow definition, and white for the brightest highlight detail. Once you have built up a collection, divide them into small separate containers according to the various colour groups most frequently used in life studies – browns, pinks, 'flesh' colours, creams, greys, black – since it will ease selection as you work. Pastels that have become grubby and perhaps lost their identity, can be cleaned by shaking them up for a few moments in a loose bag of uncooked rice.

Before attempting a figure drawing in pastels, you should try out a few basic exercises:

(1) with square-ended pastels (break new sticks in half for ease of handling), practise using end-on, side-on and edge-on application, moving the stick in different directions to see the width and character of the marks made;

(2) practise applying pastels by gradually decreasing the pressure from heavy to light and observe the variations in density and colour;

(3) using the flat side of the stick, practise wide, sweeping movements to create arc-shaped marks. In attempting to describe much of the nude figure, this arc-like rendering is essential;

(4) select a range of soft-toned colours – white, grey, lilac, pink, cream, beige and sand – and try them out both singly and overlapping in a variety of permutations on a selection of different coloured paper – white, cream, grey, fawn, brown and black. This will demonstrate to you the effect the paper has on colour combinations.

To begin a life study in coloured pastels, apply them lightly in definite strokes, making use of either the end or the side of the sticks, following the main planes of the form as you might for a drawing in monochrome pastels or charcoal, but identifying colour variations as well as tonal ones. Draw quite large and block in the whole figure as rapidly as possible in order to capture the essence of the pose. Providing you work without pressing too hard, you will always be able to correct and re-correct the proportions as the drawing progresses.

The human figure is full of the most exquisitely subtle colour combinations and to get any approximation of these you should allow each colour to 'bleed' through the one on top. This is one of the reasons for applying the pigment with a light pressure. Look for those areas that pick up and reflect colours from elsewhere – whether it be from the background drapes, cushions or props. If light is falling from more than one direction, this will create pools of reflected light and colour. Peripheral vision is important here. Try to look slightly to one side of the model while still retaining the overall colour pattern of the figure. You will find shadows in particular are made up from blue, green and mauve shades as well as the more obvious brown and grey.

When beginning a pastel drawing, the whole figure should be blocked in with light, definite strokes, allowing each colour to 'bleed' through the next layer. (*11 x 17 in/ 28 x 43 cm*)

It is important to capture a dynamic composition as quickly as possible. (*Pastels 19 x 15 in/48 x 38 cm*)

Whatever colour you are handling at any given moment, try, by closer and closer observation of your subject, to ascertain where else that colour could be applied. It is both inhibiting and time-consuming to keep changing your colours for each and every statement. The more of the overall pattern of colours you are able to block in, the more dynamic a composition you will achieve. Then, as you gradually refine the drawing, you can be more precise in colour selection. Before using each pastel you select, first test it on a scrap of the same paper as your drawing to be sure it is the colour you want.

As your drawing progresses and nears completion, avoid it becoming accidentally smudged by using a mahlstick to rest on and immediately a drawing is finished, make sure it cannot be damaged by protecting it with fixative sprayed either from an aerosol can or by diffuser.

Coloured Pencils

The technique for coloured pencils differs in a number of respects from that adopted for pastels. With pastels, because of their chalky nature, a large expanse can be covered more quickly and thoroughly than with pencils. Although, like their graphite equivalent, the latter can be sharpened to a long point allowing the side of the cone to be used as well as the tip, this cannot be expected to fill in a large area easily and rapidly as effectively as a pastel stick. By the same token a single stroke will not make as thick and opaque a mark as that from pastels. This limited covering power may prompt an artist to elect to draw on a smaller scale than might otherwise be the case with pastels.

Coloured pencils are available in a variety of qualities, some more or less greasy or chalky than others. One type is made with pastel compound. The range of colours is vast and pencils can be purchased singly or in a variety of sets from six upwards. There are some boxed collections which have as many as 72 assorted colours – far more than perhaps any water-colourist or oil-painter would ever choose to have on their palette. Working on life studies, artists may wish to avoid the confusion of too much choice, not to mention cost, by restricting the range to no more than, say, 12–18 selected for their harmony and appropriateness for flesh tones. Make sure there is a range of tones as well as colours, choosing where possible lighter and darker tones of the same colours.

An assortment of pencils within the sanguine/brown range chosen for their close harmony are ideal for life studies and portraits. By using just six colours: brown ochre, Venetian red, terracotta, chocolate, white and possibly black, on a grey-toned Ingres paper, a wonderfully delicate blending of graduated tones can be achieved. They are manufactured not only with a standard round stock but also in flat 'carpenter's pencil' form which gives a broader mark as well as a thinner one. A light application should be used, gradually building layer upon layer, and only in clear-cut details should any real pressure be adopted.

Coloured pencils with sharp points allow details of features to be more crisply defined.
(*14 x 9 in/35.5 x 23 cm*)

The sanguine/brown range of pencils gives a natural harmony to portraits and life studies. *(20 x 15 in/51 x 38 cm)*

Begin by lightly sketching in the whole figure or portrait head with ochre. Now attempt to model the warmer areas gently with terracotta, followed by shadow areas in Venetian red. Take special note of the background tones and without defining any particular objects establish the contrast between the tones in the subject and those behind. White can now be applied to emphasize the highlighted planes and finally chocolate brown for the deepest shadow detail. Black can sometimes be used for any really dense, cooler shadows. Once the first graduations have been applied, continue adjusting the weight of tone by alternately employing combinations of light on dark and dark on light. White will significantly alter the character of the darker colours.

Some ranges of coloured pencils are water-soluble. These can be used firstly by the customary method, followed by gradual blending with a watercolour brush and clean water. Alternatively, clean water can be applied to areas of the paper into which the pencil can be deployed, allowing the colour to spread. For subsequent work on the drawing both systems can be used.

Watercolour

Watercolour is a medium about which scores of books have been written. It can involve techniques and subtleties that may take years to accomplish. It can be crafted like no other medium, employing dampened paper and thin washes gradually built up from the very lightest to the very darkest areas. For life drawing, though, where a polished result is less important than the activity itself, the constraints need not be quite so rigid. It can also be great fun and artistically very rewarding.

Choose good quality artists' materials: artists' watercolours in whole-pan or half-pan sizes or in tubes, sable or imitation sable brushes, and a specialist watercolour paper such as Bockingford or Whatman, or a watercolour board.

The reason for using a specialist paper is that, owing to the amount of wetting it receives, it requires maximum strength in its structure and a surface that will not easily become scuffed. Cartridge and similar papers are unable to withstand such treatment without breaking down and eventually disintegrating. Watercolour board (a watercolour paper with a strong backing material) can be worked on without any further treatment, although it can be made more secure by taping it on to a drawing board.

Watercolour paper should be 'stretched' on a drawing board by first soaking it in clean water, laying it flat on the board and then gently wiping away the residue water to exclude as much air as possible. Seal the edges all round with gummed strip and leave the paper to drain and dry for several hours, preferably overnight, although the process can be speeded up by using a hair-drier. The final result should be a taut and

Stretched hand-made paper and artists' quality materials are essential for a watercolour life study.

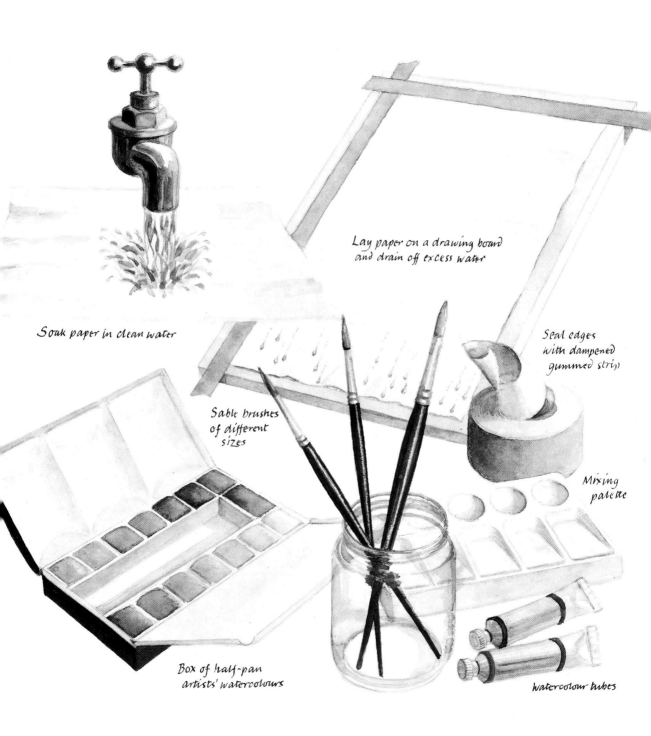

Lay paper on a drawing board
and drain off excess water

Soak paper in clean water

Seal edges
with dampened
gummed strip

Sable brushes
of different
sizes

Mixing
palette

Box of half-pan
artists' watercolours

Watercolour tubes

flattened surface which will thereafter take any number of colour washes without cockling. A good quality paper will also allow a certain amount of washing out of unwanted areas using a sponge (a natural one, though expensive, is by far the best), and will even withstand a little scraping once the surface is dry.

The pigments should be kept as clean as possible and their application as light as possible for as long as possible by using plenty of fresh clean water. In areas where the tap water is particularly hard, there can be an adverse effect on the colours and it may be advisable to use purified water obtainable from a chemist or garage.

Some artists like to begin a watercolour by pencilling in the basic outline of the figure. If this approach is adopted, it must be done with as few lines as necessary and very, very lightly applied, otherwise the pencil marks will not only show through the surface of the transparent colour, but may even get in the way of any attempt to adjust the underlying drawing.

Alternatively, you can use the watercolour very wet and quite faint for direct blocking in. Use as large a brush as possible for this and sketch in either the positive shape of the figure, or the negative shape of the background in just clean water. Then, with your brush fully charged with some diluted pigment of a light tone, allow the paint to spread over the blocked-in area. Have a sponge ready to mop up any runs and spreads you do not want. It may be necessary to tilt your board to a more horizontal position to prevent serious runs. Gradually build your drawing with thin layers of colour registering the planes and the forms of the figure and the background. It is not an ideal medium for graduating the roundness of a limb as might be done with coloured pencils. This has to be done by the application of separate translucent layers either wet on wet or wet on dry.

Depending on the degree of detail you may wish to develop, you should choose brushes of various sizes, but try to use them in decreasing order of size so that you are not tempted to become engrossed in the details before the overall pose is fully explored and established. Be aware of the highlight areas so that you do not inadvertently allow any pigment to encroach on them. Trying to get back to white paper once an area is covered can be laboriously difficult.

There are differing views regarding the range of colours that might be required. Some artists prefer a full range right across the spectrum in order to develop the techniques mastered by the Impressionists and Post-Impressionists. Others recommend a limited range restricted to, say, eight or ten hues chosen to exploit a natural harmony. It is entirely a matter of choice and individuals should experiment with both styles.

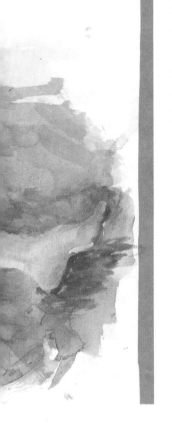

A watercolour should be kept as light as possible for as long as possible.
(8 x 18 in/20 x 46 cm)

Part 3
FURTHER OBSERVATIONS

'Lord, grant that I may always desire more than I can accomplish.'

– Michelangelo

Nothing worthwhile is ever achieved without taking risks. Drawing from a life model is no exception since, at its core, this is not a cosy, comfortable activity that becomes easier each time it is performed. What finally gives more satisfaction: repeating something you knew you could do, or stretching yourself to achieve something you thought you could not do? Be prepared to take that courageous step into the unknown which is the prerequisite of any form of original creativity. To this end it is worthwhile experimenting with different media, different sizes of drawing, different lighting effects, different viewpoints, different timescales – anything that will heighten perceptive awareness and help to develop originality of concept.

In drawing, creativity is the antithesis of copying, the process of going through the same motions over and over, superficially reproducing a drawing without getting to its heart. To overcome this, each new drawing you start should be treated as though it were the *first* one – a unique moment of discovery and invention. Let the subject itself guide and direct the way and never be afraid of spoiling your work. The important point is to let go of the security of those aspects with which you feel comfortable and begin to experience the joy of breaking down the barriers to your own progress. As the philosopher Alfred Whitehead said, 'Art flourishes where there is a sense of adventure.'

Pictorial Composition

Composition can be a strong feature even in a ten-minute sketch. (*Pastels 11 x 9 in/28 x 23 cm*)

Composition is not an easy concept to grasp, and it is almost too intangible to define precisely. As Dr Johnson said when asked what poetry is, 'It is much easier to say what it is not. We all *know* what light is; but it is not easy to *tell* what it is.'

Opposite Pictorial composition is a blend of tensions, rhythms and tonal values. (*Coloured pencils on grey paper 15 x 12 in/ 38 x 30.5 cm*)

Right The basic pattern of the composition should be established early on in the drawing. (*Sepia wash highlighted with white chalk 17 x 12 in/43 x 30.5 cm*)

Pictorial composition is to some extent the completeness of shape, a formal arrangement where every stroke helps to bring everything together to engage and hold the viewer's attention. It is a blend of tensions and climaxes, of rhythms, patterns and tonal values, often directed to centre on one or several closely connected focal points. Whenever these objectives are fulfilled, the result is self-contained visual excitement, fusion and completeness.

Compositional drawing can be likened to the conducting of a symphony orchestra. Just as the conductor must be aware of the whole musical composition at all times – its pattern, rhythms, volume, stresses, harmony, melody, counterpoints and tonality, so the draughtsman should be conscious of his entire subject without giving undue attention to one small area to the exclusion of everything else. And just as the musical director needs to be sensitive to what each part of the orchestra is playing at any given moment, so the artist needs to be sensitive to all parts of the figure whatever statement he then happens to be making.

By taking an overview of the complete subject, relating each small part to every other part and trying to remain focused on the entire model while drawing any specific feature, you will learn to see the whole and not just the sum of its various parts. This is the only way to achieve any kind of overall harmony of composition.

Establish a central focal point to your composition and attempt to revolve all the marks you make around it in such a way that visually they are eventually brought back to that point of departure. Try to be conscious of the linear rhythms and tonal patterns in an abstract way. See where the stronger contours and the shadows of folds and creases appear to run into each other as though following a pre-set path. Be selective and where they help to consolidate the composition, remember to incorporate any props or background features. Once this basic design has been established, your attention can be allowed to dwell on the other fundamentals – structure, form and texture. But never lose sight of the basic compositional design.

Lighting

The intensity, direction and quality of lighting on the nude figure are some of the principal methods by which the mood of the life class is influenced. All too often poses are set up with all available lights blazing. This may be ideal if your only objective is to see every minute detail, each wrinkle, toenail and eyelash, as clearly as possible. But in order to establish a more sympathetic and exciting atmosphere, it is far better to be a little more imaginative in both reducing the total amount of overall light and where possible adjusting its direction.

Warm daylight brings out both form and colour in the nude figure. (*Pastels 16 x 11 in/40.5 x 28 cm*)

Probably the most perfect lighting arrangement of all is that of daylight – preferably diffused – illuminating the model from more or less one direction only. Some secondary, reflected light will almost always be apparent however strong and direct the main source is. When such conditions are available, experiment with the position of the model in relation to the light source. Consider placing the nude at some distance from a window so that there is no direct sunlight playing over the form; but then also try placing the model very close to a window, even to the extent of creating a silhouette, which can be visually dramatic and very exciting to draw. Remember though, there is one important drawback: daylight is fugitive. The sun may be in or out, pale or bright, and of course it changes in intensity and direction throughout the course of the day. However, for drawings taking only one or two hours, there is nothing better.

When artificial light is used, as is most often the case, do not necessarily be content with a basic overall illumination, but instead try out various combinations of the available equipment. If there are only overhead lights which are switched on singly or in groups, experiment with partial

Side lighting not only makes the form more evident but also creates a dramatic atmosphere. (*Black and white pastels: left 20 x 14 in/51 x 35.5 cm; right 16 x 9 in/40.5 x 23 cm*)

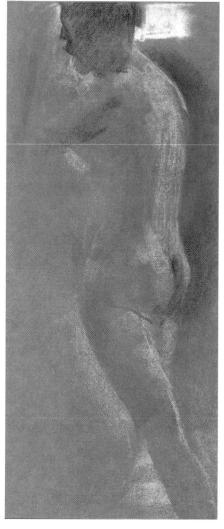

lighting. Similarly with adjustable spotlights, carry out tests both for direction and intensity. Very intense lighting from one side creates the dramatic contrasts that in drawing and painting is known as *chiaroscuro*. A few minutes spent modifying the lighting can considerably improve the next three hours' activity.

One exercise worth trying is to draw three or four versions of the same pose from the same viewpoint but each time using a different lighting arrangement or intensity. It is surprising how different the figure can appear under a variety of lighting conditions. Be really adventurous and create quite dramatic effects by sometimes having all the lights directed from one side, or from quite low down. Some of the best studies by both

A light source behind the model can be tackled with the simplest of statements rapidly made. (*Black and white pastels on grey paper: left 18 x 13 in/46 x 33 cm; right 19 x 13 in/48 x 33 cm*)

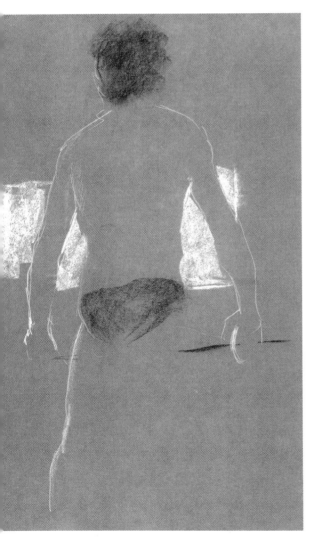

Degas and Toulouse-Lautrec were largely influenced by the dramatic underlighting of their subjects at the Parisian ballet and the cabaret. If it is night-time, turn off all the lights except those trained on the model. You will find there is usually enough 'bounced' light around by which to see your drawing. By emphasizing different aspects of the subject and the setting, this exercise prompts you to see with fresh eyes each time, literally and metaphorically to see things in a different light. It is particularly beneficial if you can arrange all the drawings in a harmonious way on a single sheet of paper. But do try to keep them all to scale.

Directional lighting such as a spotlight is also a useful tool in the study of anatomical features. In order to isolate the surface muscles and bones visually (*see* Basic Anatomy, page 32), the light can be positioned and directed across the form in such a way that strong shadows more clearly define the structure.

Silhouettes

A development in the creative use of lighting is the deliberate staging of a life pose in silhouette, or as near to it as is practicable. While our attempts at capturing this on paper need be neither as precise nor so contrived as the extremely painstaking cut-out versions fashionable during the eighteenth and nineteenth centuries, drawing in silhouette is one of the means by which the student can observe and recreate the overall shape of the figure without being concerned, initially at least, with form and texture or with becoming immersed in the detail. Of course this is not to say that a successfully executed silhouette does not contain the inherent suggestion of these other elements within its superficially flattened shape, but they are not the prime purpose of the study. The benefits to be gained will be found in that, by eliminating all but the essential shapes of head, torso and limbs, their relationship to each other and to the background are all the more clearly perceived and understood. Seeing and describing the simple essence of the pose is what matters most in this exercise.

The model should be positioned against a simple, uncluttered background such as a wall, screen or curtain, which should be as white or light-coloured as possible. The background only must be illuminated

Strong directional lighting
can be used to emphasize
anatomical features.
(*Pastels 19 x 11 in/
48 x 28 cm*)

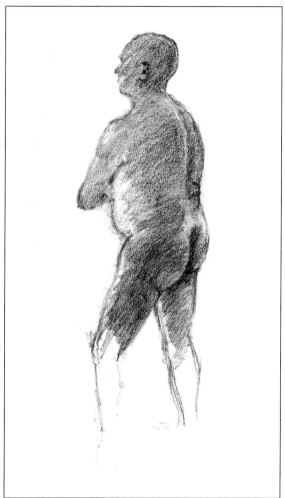

with as little spillage on to the body as possible. A window through which bright daylight is streaming can be the ideal situation. Of course, in order for everyone to see their own drawings a certain amount of light will inevitably appear in front of the model, but it is essential to keep this to an absolute minimum, otherwise the effect will be lost.

Students who have become accustomed to outlining the contour of the figure should now take this opportunity to draw in a broad, flat treatment. Charcoal or the flat side of a pastel stick are prime materials with which to render either the shape of the figure on a white ground or the shape around the figure on a dark ground. Paint or ink can both also be used for this simplified image-making, but only with a broad brush. Speed, too, is important in order to avoid the temptation to elaborate.

Three examples of silhouette drawings: white pencil on black paper (*12 x 8 in/ 30.5 x 20 cm*); graphite pencil (*19 x 10 in/48 x 25.5 cm*); and, making use of natural light, sepia wash highlighted with chalk on toned paper (*11 x 10 in/ 28 x 25.5 cm*).

Drawing Details

Drawing *a* detail is different from drawing *in* detail. The first refers to selecting and isolating one feature of the model to the exclusion of all others, whereas the second alludes to the inclusion of the minutiae of the subject. The most obvious example of the former is in the making of a portrait, but this is such a major subject in its own right, it has been given its own subject heading. There are several other parts of the body which can be selected as suitable subjects for individual attention: hands, feet, torso, legs and so on. And to draw some of them does not necessarily require the model to be a nude. The main purpose in taking these features out of context is twofold. Firstly, in the course of drawing the

whole figure there is usually little or no time to pay enough attention to individual details; they often get a rather cursory treatment – particularly features like ears and eyes. Secondly, it is a rare opportunity for you to bring a drawing up to a high state of finish, which in itself can be both challenging and very satisfying.

Apart from the face, the most expressive parts of the human body are the hands. We use our hands as instrumental tools for thousands of different activities every day from the delicately precise to the robustly coarse. But, by the enlistment of a wide range of expressive gestures, we also use them to augment ideas in conversation. Watch any two or more people holding a conversation and you cannot fail to notice how often the hands are used to describe and emphasize various points. In the paintings of Nicolas Poussin, the seventeenth-century classical French artist, the hands of his subjects are as expressive as their faces. The power of gesture is such that even when talking on the telephone we sometimes accentuate points with our free hand which is impossible for the other person to see. For all serious students of figure drawing it is therefore crucially important to make studies of hands in many different positions: open, clenched, grasping objects, delicately folded, gesturing and so forth, and from as many different viewpoints as possible. It has been said that if you can draw hands, you can draw anything and to get the maximum benefit demands a high degree of concentrated observation.

Begin by dividing each hand into simplified angles and planes and do not at first try to separate the fingers. Take note how long the back of the hand is between the wrist joint and the first line of knuckles. Remember that the fingers are not simply skins filled like sausages, but are made up from intricately jointed bones and muscles which have already been briefly examined under Basic Anatomy, page 36. Observe how the three sets of joints are arranged; notice how far the fingers and wrists actually bend, both when relaxed and when clenched. Try to analyse the complementary relationship of the concave palm inside and the convex knuckles outside. Also be aware that hands are almost as personal as faces and each model's has individual characteristics of shape, size, texture and colour.

Feet, too, are notoriously difficult to draw and require intense efforts of analysis to achieve a semblance of realism. With proper regard for the perspective, once again try to break down the problem into its various

It is important to make studies of individual features such as hands and feet which may not receive enough attention when drawing the whole figure. (*Graphite pencil 22 x 16 in/56 x 40.5 cm*)

components of planes and angles. Imagine the simplified stages a foot would need to go through if it were being carved out of stone, and then, stage by stage, very gradually reveal the complexity of each individual element. Refer to the anatomical breakdown if there is something in the structure you do not understand.

Other features that, when taken out of context, can be both demanding and rewarding to the draughtsman are ears and eyes. Although everyone has the same anatomical parts, no two people have ears of the same shape or size so you cannot entirely rely on previous experience. Each model has to be studied anew. See, for instance, how ears are partially inset into the head and partially protruding from it. They are extremely complex structures which take a great deal of determined examination to convey them accurately to paper. But start by breaking them down into convenient and controllable parts.

Eyes also create special problems for the artist. But study them with care and think of them essentially as hooded balls set into their sockets. Try not to become too confused by all the intricate details of eyelids and pupils. These can be left until the final stages of your drawing. By breaking the problems down into manageable 'sight-bites' they become less daunting. And once you have become familiar with studying these isolated items of detail in detail, you will find you can more easily put them into context when you attempt a portrait or whole figure.

Portrait Heads

Quite understandably, most students drawing a portrait will wish above all else to achieve a likeness of the sitter and it is possible to render a relatively superficial likeness by means of selecting the most characteristic features, rather in the way a caricaturist operates. It is almost certainly more beneficial, though, to persevere with getting the construction right first before applying any personal identification to the face. Think initially about the skull beneath the skin and the way it fits as an extension and culmination of the spinal column from which it receives the mechanism enabling it to tilt and turn. It could justifiably be claimed that there are just as many personality traits in these simple functions of the head as there are in the shape of the nose and the colour of the eyes.

Imagine your drawing as if it were being modelled by gradual applications of layers on to the underlying structure: first the skull, then the flesh and muscle, then the hair and finally the mouth, ears and eyes. Keep measuring, reading across and relating each feature against several others: depth of forehead; width of eyes; alignment of ears to nose, mouth to chin and so on; how the hair grows from the surface of the skull and is not merely set upon it like a cap. In this way a more fundamental and honest portrait will emerge, not simply a mimic of the original.

The face reflects much of the character and personality. Try to be sensitive to those intangible qualities which make each of us a unique human being. Over a period of several hours the features of a sitter may slacken and, perhaps due to fatigue or boredom or maybe simply

To achieve a likeness of the sitter requires getting the construction right as well as putting features in the right places. (*Left charcoal 23 x 16 in/58.5 x 40.5 cm; right black and white pastel pencils on grey paper 14 x 11 in/35.5 x 28 cm*)

through becoming lost in their own thoughts, appear bland and devoid of their initial spark of personality. Photographs can sometimes capture a moment that exemplifies the individuality of a person because the shutter clicks in a hundredth of a second. While artists are not trying to compete in that way, it is important to retain that essential spark of life in a portrait.

Very few portraits show a laughing or even smiling expression. Where they do, it is most likely to have been interpreted from photographic evidence – and often looks like it. Copying from photographs can never be a substitute for working with a model. Possibly one answer to the problem is to engage the sitter in conversation at vital moments so that their attention is regained and vitality renewed. The eyes are particularly expressive in this regard – they are sometimes called the windows of the soul – and must be tackled with great sensitivity. One crucial aspect to consider is the focusing of the eyes, so make a conscious effort to draw both eyes at the same time. This is not only to ensure that you have established their common point of focus but also by reading across in this way, you will more accurately position them within the face.

In a portrait study both eyes should be drawn at the same time to achieve accurate alignment and focus. (*Sepia wash: left 14 x 11 in/35.5 x 28 cm; right 12 x 9 in/30.5 x 23 cm*)

The mouth also carries a lot of personal identity and should be examined with intense care. Do not be in too great a rush to draw the division between the lips but study first the surrounding structure of those areas just below the nose, above the chin and where the cheeks on either side impinge on the corners of the mouth. By building the feature within its surroundings in this way, you will achieve a much more accurate understanding of it. It is the bone structure and muscle formation that makes the mouth, not the other way round. The mouth follows the shape of the face and the underlying structure of the maxilla and mandible bones.

Timed Studies

Studies produced to a time limit of one minute, five minutes or ten minutes, encourage the artist to draw in a direct, swift manner helping to overcome any inherent diffidence. This is not a matter of arrogance or over-confidence but rather a means of stating what you see in the simplest of terms. There is no time for a careful, considered and exacting study. That can be left for another occasion (*see* Planning and Building, page 15). But to capture the essence of an action or posture, when there may be only the briefest of moments in which to react, be bold and straightforward. Isolate the essentials: the stance, the direction of the spinal column, the incline of the head, the angle of the limbs and the compositional rhythm. Reduce the whole study to nothing more than basic patterns and movements.

To get the best from this exercise, it is advisable to use a broad medium such as charcoal, pastel or watercolour wash, but if a pencil is preferred, then the side of the graphite of a soft grade should be used.

Because the model is not being asked to hold any one position for more than a few minutes, exciting action poses can be devised. Try to persuade the model to take on a dynamic sporting posture such as throwing a javelin or discus (which has a long pedigree in art history as far back as Classical Greece), or a dramatic one, including strong facial expressions. I have occasionally found that 'resting' actors, also working as life models, are very good for these sessions. If you are very fortunate, you may get a professional dancer modelling who is prepared to demonstrate dance positions or balances. Less exotic but perhaps just as

Poses set for rapid one- and two-minute sketches are often dynamic so the style of drawing should be equally vigorous. (*Pastels on dark blue paper: left 18 x 12 in/46 x 30.5 cm; right 17 x 8 in/43 x 20 cm*)

exciting to draw are everyday activities like reaching for a high shelf, bending to lift something from the floor or simply pointing at some distant object. Although possibly somewhat stressful for the model, the duration of these poses is very brief, and in my experience, on the whole models quite enjoy the challenge and the chance to be creative. They also welcome the opportunity to take on a number of poses rather than just one long one which can be more tiring to hold.

Inevitably in setting these rapid time poses, everyone is under a good deal of pressure to capture the basics before the model moves. It is, therefore, recommended only doing them for half an hour or so in any one session. Also, except for the sequence poses, the lengths of time should

Left Even a fairly standard pose takes on a lively appearance when drawn in just a few minutes. (*Graphite pencil highlighted with white pencil 18 x 14 in/ 46 x 35.5 cm*)

Right The results of drawing without looking at the paper can be surprisingly full of energy. (*Pencil 16 x 11 in/40.5 x 28 cm*)

always be announced in advance and should be varied between one minute and ten minutes. Towards the end of each pose it is helpful to state that there is either one minute or two minutes to go. One of the objectives in setting poses for a variety of predetermined times is to enable students to begin to appreciate how much can be accomplished in any given length of time; to learn how to pace a drawing. A one-hour drawing is not simply a five-minute drawing extended to fill the time available: they have quite different purposes and approaches.

One final 'fun' exercise to end a sequence in a more relaxed way is to draw from an action pose for two minutes without actually looking at the paper. By fixing the focus only on the model a more direct and

continuous application is encouraged which very often results in a surprisingly effective drawing. Without lifting your hand, keep the point of
your pencil on the paper and simply 'take it for a walk', or even a run!

(*See also* Props, page 121)

Spatial Awareness

For the draughtsman, form and volume are reasonably simple concepts
to grasp. A more difficult concept when drawing from a model is the
existence of that form and volume in space with air circulating around it.
There is space between you and the model; there is space between the
model and any other artists drawing from the same pose; there is space
between all objects in the studio; there is space between the four walls of
the room. Human beings are blessed in having binocular vision. That is
the ability to judge distances and see around objects directly in front of
us which we owe to the position and alignment of our eyes on a plane at
the front of the face and to their focusing in unison. You can get some
idea of how limited our vision might be if each eye worked independent-
ly by closing one and trying to estimate how far away any chosen object
is. It is tantamount to seeing two-dimensionally as opposed to seeing
three-dimensionally.

As explained earlier, 'negative shapes' are the apparent spaces
between limbs and various other parts of the body seen primarily in a
two-dimensional way. Try now to bring your mind to the negative
spaces that appear around, between, over and under different parts of a
model in a three-dimensional way. By applying your binocular vision
you will begin to appreciate that the figure lives and breathes in space
and that there is also a spatial relationship between you and the model.

An exercise to bring this concept into better focus is to surround the
model with any number of large standing objects such as spare easels,
standing spotlights, chairs, plants, indeed anything that will partially
mask your viewpoint. Since you cannot simply ignore these objects as
you attempt to draw you will soon become more conscious of the distances between them and the model and, in turn, of the space between
yourself and the model. It is axiomatic that you then become more aware
of space in relation to all things.

Awareness of objects
around the model enables
you to see the figure
within three-dimensional
space. (*Pastels 17 x 14 in/
43 x 35.5 cm*)

You will probably find that this exercise is best undertaken using a tonal medium rather than a linear one. Objects that are near appear more sharply in focus and more deeply shadowed than those that are further away, and this will become more apparent by making a series of tonal statements. Perspective also has a bearing on the relationships between the objects and the model. It pays to take the occasional measurement to see how large or small each part is to the other. After a while, test your own clarity of observation by seeing whether you can tell the distance between an object in front of you and the model beyond just by looking at your drawing. Then check just how accurate your judgement was.

Images in Time and Space

A development combining the exercises in Timed Studies, page 91, and Spatial Awareness, above, requires a number of related quick studies to be shown in a sequence of movements on the same drawing. For instance, ask the model to move in a curve across the floor, step up on to a dais, turn and stand or sit down. Each step should be held for five or six minutes so that the whole action can be 'freeze-framed' in six or seven sketches. Attempt to keep all the studies in sequence and to the same proportion, overlapping them if necessary. The important point is to capture the feeling of movement and progression through space and time. A lot can be learned about the balance and transference of weight from one foot to the other, as well as what happens to the hips, shoulders and arms.

Let the model carry out the exercise at walking speed two or three times before taking up each position for drawing. You, and the model, will then obtain a better idea of how it looks and feels. It also provides an opportunity to plan how the group of drawings is to be positioned on your paper. So that each stage can be related in both perspective and proportion, it may be necessary to show some elements of the background.

Transcribing to paper the understanding of space around a model may be achieved more easily with a series of tonal statements. (*Pastels 19 x 15 in/ 48 x 38 cm*)

Another experiment in combining space and time is to prepare a series of drawings of a model posing in the centre of the studio at four different locations each for about 15 to 20 minutes and in more or less the same stance, whether standing or seated. The objectives – and the benefits – of this exercise are several and various, but only if all four images are grouped on one sheet of paper. To do this requires planning and visualizing how the finished result might appear if there were four separate models posing at the same time.

First arrange where the four positions are going to be set by asking the model to take up each position for just a few seconds. Having established the extremities of the composition, you should then quickly and lightly sketch in three or four background features which can be used as constant reference points so that each drawing will not only be relatively placed in scale with the background but also in scale with each other. At least one of these reference points must be at your own eye level, one below and one above in order to achieve the correct perspective.

As each drawing in turn emerges, there will almost certainly be some overlapping. Do not let this worry you. Those furthest from your viewpoint should be rendered with slightly less strength of tone as they would be if there were indeed four models present. Your drawing of

A series of drawings progressively recording the movement of a model can test the imagination as well as the powers of perception. (Pastels 13 x 18 in/ 33 x 46 cm)

those nearest to you may need to 'bleed' off the top and bottom of the sheet because of the acute perspective. It is a challenge to the imagination of how the final drawings might appear making demands on the powers of observation and composition. Both memory and foresight are involved as well as an appreciation of the figures in space.

When the model poses for several minutes in each of four different places it challenges the artist's ability to foresee and plan a composition. (*Black and white pastel pencils 20 x 13 in/51 x 33 cm*)

A number of poses can be similarly adapted for multiple image drawing. Try posing the model in a standing position holding one hand on a substantial vertical item such as an easel or standing spotlight. After 15 minutes' drawing, ask the model to move round to the other side with the same hand on the vertical so that you can repeat the drawing from another angle. This can be similarly done in any number of incremental positions so that the final group of figures represents a complete circuit. In your drawing, however, you should not attempt to group more than two of them around the same upright; otherwise there would be too much confusing overlap.

Breaking Barriers and Boundaries

Any changes in method or medium can result in benefiting the artist by helping to break down some of our inhibitions and the tendencies we have of replicating the same drawing over and over again. We all experience periods when our work seems jaded and lacking any kind of development, when barriers appear to be restricting our motivation. While recognition of the malaise is the first step to overcoming it, the second step is not so obvious. Somehow we need to devise some stimulant to refresh the muse and this requires a new point of departure.

One way of instilling a new sense of drama and vigour into your drawing is by intentionally making the figure too large for the paper on which you are working. Running your drawing off three or all four edges creates a wholly new robust composition which occurs simply because it has been released from the normal confines of the paper. This exercise will encourage a broader and much more dynamic approach to your work. For this purpose, in addition to portraying the whole of the torso and shoulders, try also extracting quite a small area of, say, the abdomen and hips, or a small part of the thigh and knee. This is not intended to be the same as taking a detail to study in depth, but a way of deliberately blowing up a limited portion of the human body until it becomes almost like a landscape or an abstract drawing. This technique, together with viewing the nude from unusual angles, was brilliantly exploited by the draughtsman/photographer Man Ray. Even Picasso, the greatest of all modernists, expressed the view that, 'There is no

The human form, either in whole or in part, seen from an unusual angle can be interpreted in an almost abstract way. (*Charcoal 24 x 22 in/61 x 56 cm*)

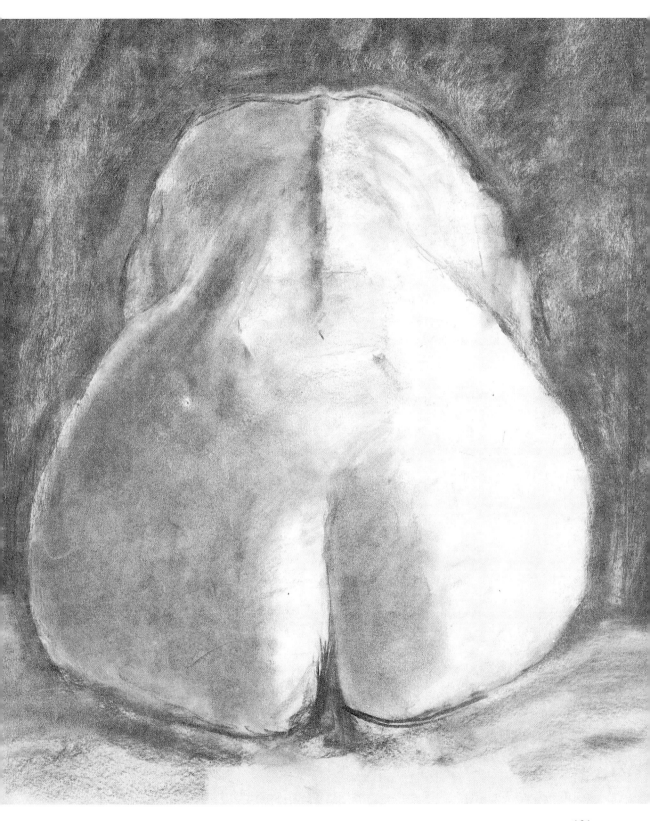

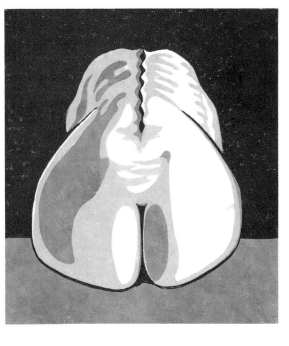

This three-colour lino print
was adapted from the
drawing on page 101.
(*9 x 8 in/23 x 20 cm*)

A pencil line drawing can be
made with the specific purpose
of translating it into a wood
engraving or scraper-board.
(*8 x 6 in/20 x 15 cm*)

abstract art, you must always start with something.' Spend some time investigating and establishing the abstract patterns in both the two-dimensional shapes and the three-dimensional form.

Drawing for Reference

Reacting and responding to the immediate inspiration of the moment is most often the reason for drawing from a life model and is essentially what this book is about. In other words, it is 'drawing for its own sake'. However, a life class can be used as a preparation for later further development of the subject. Drawing for future use prompts you to study more intently and to ask yourself more probing questions about your subject. You might like to think of it in the same terms as the note-taking you might carry out in preparation for an essay or speech. You will require as much information as possible from which to extract and select material for the final work.

For example, a sculptor intending to model or carve a figure or bust might wish to make a number of working drawings from different angles and perhaps include notes about specific features that might later be needed for establishing personal characteristics. A piece of sculpture takes a relatively long time to execute so the sitter cannot be expected to be constantly available throughout the duration of the work. In these circumstances the sculptor would need to view the pose from at least four sides and possibly from both above and low down as well, and might choose to make separate detailed notations of hands or head. Think of all the different bits of information a sculptor would need to record in order to make a clay replica or stone carving subsequently from these preparatory sketches. Although you may personally never intend to make a portrait or figure in the round, this preparatory exercise is a useful one and by setting out the drawings on to one sheet of paper, they can appear most attractive. Try to divide up the available time so that each viewpoint is given equal attention.

A graphic designer, illustrator or print-maker might need to make a drawing with a specific planned interpretation and final technique in mind. For example, the finished work may be intended for reproduction in a restricted number of printings, or in flat colours with no graduated

When drawing a clothed
figure it is important to
envisage the form beneath.
(*Black, white and sanguine
pencils 18 x 12 in/
46 x 30.5 cm*)

tones. A wood engraving, where the surface of the block prints in flat black with the portions taken out remaining white, will need a preparatory drawing that can eventually be adapted and reduced to this simple but sophisticated process. It has to be engraved as a mirror image which must also be a consideration in the planning and preparation.

Once you are reasonably familiar with the life class, begin to set yourself objective tasks like these to help to stimulate a more creative approach to the subject.

The Clothed Figure

Clothed (or costumed) figure drawing is ideally and essentially a development from nude figure drawing, although studies of the former are more likely to have preceded the latter if only because of cultural and social conditions. The availability of clothed models will obviously be the factor in determining which becomes most frequently the subject for a drawing. However, to draw the dressed human body with conviction requires a good deal of knowledge about the *un*dressed human body. Only by having a clear idea of the structure and movement of the form beneath the clothing can we begin to understand and portray accurately how the stretch, hang and folds of various fabrics can be made to appear plausible. Just as in a portrait it is necessary to 'see' the skull beneath the skin, so in a clothed figure it is necessary to 'see' the form beneath the cloth. The artists who, with integrity, have studied the nude from various angles over a long period of time and in a wide range of poses, will invariably be able to drape or wrap that nude convincingly in their drawing.

One exercise which helps to appreciate the value of this precept is first to draw the figure as a nude and then repeat the drawing from the same viewpoint and under the same lighting conditions with the model dressed, or partly draped in a fabric which follows the form as much as possible. This should clearly demonstrate where and how the form dictates the stretch, hang and fold of the material. It will of course vary depending on the weight and the coarseness of the material, the looseness of the fit and the pose adopted.

Except where a garment is very close-fitting, only in certain places is the body shape visible on the outside. Try to identify these places on the model when he or she is standing, seated or reclining. For example, a loose shirt on a standing figure touches at the neck, shoulders and upper back, the waist (if it is belted) and the wrists. On a female it will probably touch at the breasts as well. When the arm is bent, it will also touch at the elbow. In all other places the underlying form remains almost anonymous. Much depends on the fullness of the figure but these examples generally apply.

Trousers on a seated figure normally define the shape of the thigh, knee and back of the lower leg showing pronounced stretch folds from the knee to the back of the thigh and down the front of the lower leg. Sleeves show a similar presence of stretch folds from the bent elbow down to the wrist and up to the shoulder.

Left Sensitive appreciation of the texture of the fabric will eventually become manifest in the drawing. (*Pastels 13 x 10 in/ 33 x 25.5 cm*)

Opposite Creases and folds are evidence of particular stresses caused by the body's activity or posture. (*Charcoal 23 x 17 in/ 58.5 x 43 cm*)

A hat can enhance a portrait but it must be seen to encompass the volume of the head beneath. (*Charcoal 16 x 12 in/40.5 x 30.5 cm*)

Different fabrics display different textures, even when colour is not a visual factor. Provided sufficiently sensitive attention has been paid to the surface textures of any given fabric, its representation in a figure drawing should make it identifiable. Silk, cotton, wool and denim, each have definite characteristics in both texture and weight that influence the qualities of fold, crease and hang. Velvet, for instance, is distinctive in that it presents a predominantly darkened appearance where lighter tones are restricted to the very crests of the folds. It is often only possible to see the true colour of velvet at those areas where the light is strongest.

Hats have come back into fashion in recent years, especially among the younger generation. A sitter wearing a hat can often enhance a portrait or half-figure drawing, giving it a lot of style. As with other items that clothe the figure, it is important that the artist takes account of the structure of the head beneath the hat. It should be perceived that the hollow inside precisely encompasses the volume of the skull and by initially following the inner rim around the circumference of the head (even where it runs out of sight or is masked by the brim), these relative dimensions will begin to be understood. If there is a brim or peak to the hat, the outer edge of this can next be positioned, taking account of the perspective and allowing for any waves or kinks that are visible. Finally the crown can be accurately superimposed because the framework has been so carefully plotted beforehand.

Part 4
PRACTICAL ISSUES FOR TUTORS AND STUDENTS

'The art of teaching is the art of assisting discovery.' – Mark van Doren

Locating Life Classes

Life drawing may not be a pursuit readily available to some who might otherwise be keen to try. Unless you have the resources of an established, professional painter, arranging your own studio and model is not easily accomplished. Fortunately, on the whole, this is not necessary.

In the UK many, if not most, local authorities run adult evening classes, and through some community associations day classes as well, although in recent times the financial pressures on local government budgets have sadly resulted in a somewhat reduced provision. They are usually organized on a term-by-term basis, beginning in September, January and April. Watch out for announcements in your local newspaper before each term starts or obtain a prospectus from the adult education institute nearest to your home. If there are no classes locally, ask your public library for information about any further afield.

In addition to the local authority classes some further education colleges run evening courses. It is worth making enquiries at the college admissions office. There are also a number of private art schools holding life drawing sessions, either on a one-day-a-week basis or as weekend or one-week courses. These are advertised in the arts magazines and in some of the larger artists' supply shops.

Although the dedicated artist needs nothing more than a model and some materials, additional facilities can help a life class to run efficiently. (*Two coloured pencils on brown paper 17 x 12 in/ 43 x 30.5 cm*)

Equipping the Life Studio

Very few shared-use studios, especially those run for adult or community education, will be ideally sited or fully equipped for life drawing. Municipal resources do not often stretch to the degree where such a

specialist subject is allowed to have its own exclusive accommodation. The dedicated artist will of course make do with the bare minimum of equipment, provided there is a model and something on which to draw. It is quite useful, however, to have some knowledge of what a well-appointed studio could be like.

The studio should be large enough to accommodate the numbers taking part comfortably. A reasonable area for, say, 20 students would be 1000 square feet (93 square metres) with a height of at least 10 feet (3 metres). While a studio filled with closely packed students all deeply concentrating on their drawing is exhilarating to experience, there is a point where overcrowding affects the sightlines to the model. A larger studio may well be able to accommodate a greater number of students but in order for each person to have a full view of the model, everyone would need to be that much further away, possibly to such a degree that sight-size could be unacceptably small.

Left Adjustable blinds are needed to cut out direct sunlight but they can also be used to create interesting shadows. (*Black and white pastels 14 x 11 in/ 35.5 x 28 cm*)

Right A dais, screen and a table are standard items of equipment in the life studio. (*Black and white pastels 16 x 11 in/ 40.5 x 28 cm*)

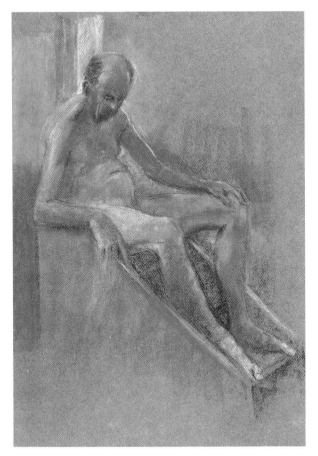

Good light is essential so there should be at least one wall of windows, preferably on the north side, with obscured glass if the studio is overlooked. If the windows are subjected to direct sunlight, there should be adjustable blinds. Where the studio is a purpose-built one, there may be skylights instead of or as well as windows, and these too may need blinds to cut out direct sunlight.

Fixtures should include a dressing cubicle for the model, a sink and running water for cleaning painting materials, several power sockets from which to run spotlights and heaters, storage space for paper, materials and props, and pinboards for displaying work.

Movable items of furniture should ideally include a dais separated into sections for flexibility of staging, a chair, table and sofa for the poses, background screens, standing spotlights, heaters for the model, and a big hamper containing a selection of coloured drapes and cushions. Another very useful item is a large mirror for occasional use as a means of

Left Portable steps are a useful piece of equipment on which to set poses. (*Pastels 18 x 14 in/ 46 x 35.5 cm*)

Right Mirrors of various sizes help to create interesting poses. (*Pastels 15 x 9 in/38 x 23 cm*)

demonstrating the back and front of a pose at one and the same time.

Equipment for work should include easels capable of taking an imperial-size drawing board, donkeys for those students who prefer to work seated, drawing boards in both imperial and half-imperial sizes and some small tables on which to rest materials beside the easels.

Life Models

Life models are booked on a sessional basis generally by the organization running the class, or by the tutor. Once a class is advertised, models and would-be models will usually apply to be placed on the register. Often, many of the younger models are themselves full-time students or ex-students supplementing their income or grant and normally like to be paid at the end of each session. It is not an easy occupation to remain as still as possible for an hour or so at a time, so whatever models are paid

Planning poses with a traditional wooden mannequin saves precious drawing time in the class. (*Left coloured pencils 16 x 10 in/40.5 x 25.5 cm; right charcoal 19 x 16 in/ 48 x 40.5 cm*)

for their pains is fully earned. Over a period of time each tutor builds up a list of models which is often passed on to colleagues at other institutes.

At the start of any life class it is important to put the model at ease, not only for the sake of civility but also so that they can feel able to give of their best work. An adequate cubicle or screened area where they can undress in privacy is essential. Their comfort should be a priority, not only in connection with how much a strain each pose may demand, but also with regard to the temperature in the studio and the allocation of rest periods. A model who is at ease is likely to display less movement over a prolonged period and is more likely to settle back into the pose after a rest break.

Generally, a seated pose can be held for longer without discomfort to the model than a standing pose, although it helps if there is something on which to lean. *(Pastels: left 19 x 13 in/48 x 33 cm; right 18 x 12 in/46 x 30.5 cm)*

What pose to set will depend on a number of factors. Very short-time poses allow for greater 'action' and can be more physically demanding (*see* Timed Studies, page 91 *and* Props, page 121). Longer-term poses need to be comfortable and relatively easy to return to after a break.

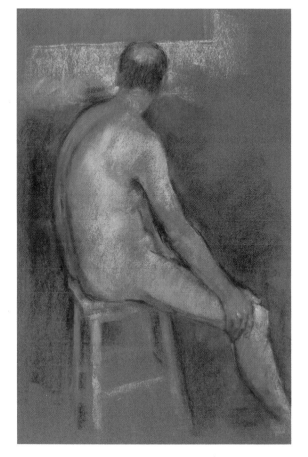

Many models need little or no direction but it helps sometimes to try out ideas for poses with a traditional artists' wooden mannequin. A little pre-planning can often save a lot of time in arranging a suitable pose during the session.

It is useful to mark certain contact points, such as the position of the feet on the floor or the hands on the chair, so that there are some points of reference when the model returns to the pose after a rest break. Also ask members of the class or group to check the pose against their own drawings after a break. It should be remembered, though, that the model may not be able to reproduce every single nuance of the original stance. Neither is it possible for the model to remain fixed in one position over a long period; the pose inevitably changes to some extent, albeit gradually and almost indiscernibly, as the tensions in the muscles relax. This presents an additional challenge to the draughtsman who must decide whether to adjust their drawing to match the pose or continue with the original. The changes are not normally so great that they present insoluble problems. As has been discussed previously, the exercise of life drawing is not to achieve a photographic likeness but to interpret the essence of the subject.

A pose is often more interesting to draw if it contains a slight twist between the ribcage and the pelvis and a further twist or incline of the head. A standing pose with the weight on one leg and the head turned creates greater drama in a composition than one where the model stands four-square. A seated pose where the side of the head or the chin is supported in one hand offers more interest than when the hands are folded together. When setting up a portrait session, try to avoid positioning the sitter looking straight out to the front. The merest turn to one side or a slight incline makes for a far better design.

Settings

Good work can be accomplished in a life class where the pose consists of nothing but the model standing on an otherwise empty dais. This basic situation consisting of the primary ingredients alone, with no extra paraphernalia, is arguably all one really needs. Repeatedly faced with the same conditions over a period of time, though, could very easily result in

A pose with a slight twist, putting more weight on one leg than the other, makes for a more interesting study. (*Three-colour pastels 17 x 11 in/43 x 28 cm*)

117

fatigue and disinterest. It is therefore to everyone's benefit sometimes to 'dress' the setting and occasionally to introduce a few of the items generally known as props.

There are two objectives in the function of dressing the set. One is to prepare a backdrop against which the model will be clearly visible, and the other is to arrange furniture and drapes on which the model can be comfortably posed. If the model is to be set up in the centre of the studio with students drawing from positions all round, then the first of these objectives is unnecessary.

Backgrounds can consist of a simple studio wall, a screen, or fabrics of one kind or another draped from a high fixture. The choice may depend not only on the availability of such items but also on factors such as the accompanying lighting, the mood required and the general overall colouring. If there is a wide choice of backgrounds, it is worthwhile spending a little time making a careful selection.

Quite exotic settings can be constructed with colourful drapes tented and swagged up behind the dais and others gathered in swathes over mounds of cushions. This kind of arrangement is particularly valuable when the pose is to be continued over an extensive period for the purpose of drawing and painting in colour. Strong colours can become

Reclining poses are of infinite variety: prone, supine, sideways, flat or curled up, and are ideal for retention over long periods. (*Left black and white pastels 12 x 10 in/30.5 x 25.5 cm; right coloured pastels 17 x 20 in/43 x 51 cm*)

overwhelming to the extent of 'killing' the more subtle tones of the flesh so, unless it is part of an exercise to show how backgrounds influence skin tones, select only subdued and harmonious colours. If potted plants are available, these too can add to the overall effect and help, by contrast and reflection, to bring out a wider range of colour tints in the flesh tones. They also create intriguing dappled shadows if placed between the model and the light source.

In a purpose-built life studio there may be a wide choice of furnishings on which to arrange the pose: chairs, stools, couches, divans, mattresses, and so on. In a multi-purpose studio the choice may be a great deal more limited. Try to make the most of the available resources. For example, it is possible to create the semblance of a couch by placing cushions on three ordinary chairs put together and draped with loose fabrics, or by spreading cushions and drapes on a dais of boxes. Whatever adaptations are made, it is of prime importance that the model should be able to feel at ease in the pose and remain comfortable for the whole of the session. This is not only for the benefit of the model, but also for the students since an uncomfortable pose makes for a fidgety model.

Props

Props such as baskets, pots, ornaments and sculptures may be selected to help to dress the set and thus be combined to make still-life and figure-drawing sessions. Or they can become more directly part of the pose. A long stick or thin pole in the hands of a suitable model can very easily assume the guise of a spear or staff. A standing pose then takes on the appearance of a warrior ready for battle. The classic subject of 'the fallen warrior' can be recreated when the same model takes up a reclining pose with his 'spear' lying across his body.

A length of rope is another adaptable prop for action poses. When secured at one end to a firm support it can be tugged from the front and pulled from over the shoulder to produce a number of powerful stances. The French painter and caricaturist, Honoré Daumier (1808–79) produced many exciting action studies like this.

To give the model something to do, however commonplace, is often better than for them merely to sit staring into space. The simple activity of reading a book, for example, can have the effect of both relaxing the model and giving the students a subject that creates a natural composition with a clear centre of interest: the relationship between the reader and the book. Another is to hold a hand mirror where again the relationship between the mirror and the eyes creates a strong composition especially advantageous to those drawing from behind the model's back.

Colouful drapes swagged up behind and around the model bring out a greater range of colours in the flesh tones. (*Pastels 18 x 12 in/46 x 30.5 cm*)

Everyday domestic activities provide perfect poses for quick sketching. 'Making the bed' is one that can be broken down into a sequence of rapid studies. It requires the minimum of resources – a dais, a sheet or similarly large piece of cloth, and a cushion. The model should be asked to hold each of these poses for no more than three or four minutes: spreading the sheet, tucking it under the mattress, plumping up the pillow and so on. If they are all drawn to the same proportion, they make a fascinating collection of studies.

Similarly, a simple bath towel used as a prop can provide an infinite number of good Degas-type poses. Brushing the hair was another subject greatly loved by Degas. A series based on 'hanging the washing' provides opportunities for bending and stretching poses and needs nothing more than a fixed cord and one or two pieces of material and a basket or bowl. There are hundreds of routine activities based on simple props that are ideal for life studies of both long and short duration.

(*See also* Timed Studies, page 91)

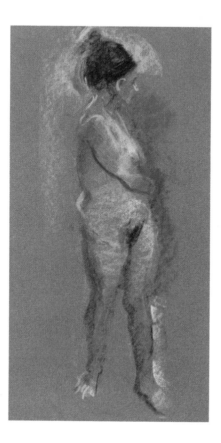

Giving the model something to do adds a dynamic element to short poses. (*Pastels 20 x 11 in/ 51 x 28 cm*)

Activity poses using sporting stances give a chance for grouping several drawings together. (*Coloured pencils with pen and ink and white chalk 18 x 12 in/ 46 x 30.5 cm*)

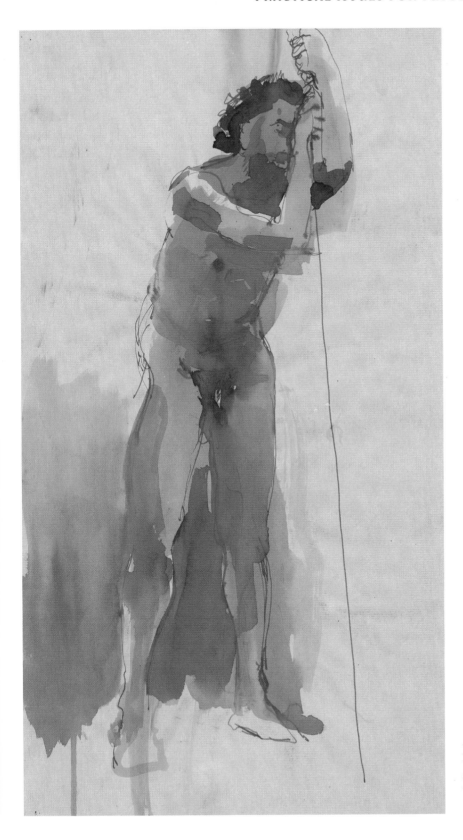

A suitable model holding a long stick can take on the guise of the exhausted warrior. (*Pen and wash 17 x 10 in/43 x 25.5 cm*)

Looking at Drawings

In addition to participating oneself in drawing from the human figure, an indispensable and deeply rewarding part of one's study is looking at the work of other artists. This includes not only the works of the great masters, but also the drawings done by peer group students in class and at exhibitions.

At the end of many of my life classes, every student is invited to display their session's work for about five minutes, for everyone else to see. All the drawings are roughly grouped together in the centre of the studio so that, while the pose is still fresh in the mind, each student can observe how others have tackled those visual problems that have been to some extent common to them all. This exercise is definitely not intended to suggest there is any competition among the class. The slightest hint of it would be contrary to the spirit of the group. The chief purpose is to demonstrate that we all see, and interpret what we see, differently – even uniquely. The secondary purpose is the reinforcement of the study as a group activity. There is an almost tangible power generated when a number of people are working together, albeit as individuals, on the same project. The combined but silent concentration can produce an electric atmosphere of creativity much greater in intensity than the sum of its individual parts. It therefore makes sense afterwards to share in the results of that united effort.

Everyone is encouraged to comment on and question the techniques, media, quality of interpretation – any aspect at all relevant to the drawings displayed. The model, too, is invited to participate in these joint discussions since he or she is an integral part of the contributing group. There is invariably a great feeling of excitement on those occasions when one member is universally recognized to have made a major breakthrough in their work. Everyone wholeheartedly shares in the pleasure of their success.

Art schools and colleges often mount annual shows of students' work, initially for the purpose of assessment but also as a 'shop window' whereby members of the public and potential employers can see the best examples produced by final-year students. These are usually held in June and July and details can be obtained from the administrative offices of each institute.

There are hundreds of galleries and museums throughout the world which house and display collections of drawings. Many of the smaller, local interest museums may have only a limited number of graphic works but these are worth seeing if you are in the vicinity. Other more important galleries may have fine collections of painting and other works of art but not very many drawings. Some galleries run by the fine art dealers as well as the large auction houses occasionally exhibit master works in advance of a sale or auction, details of which can be found advertised in the trade press or specialist magazines. Usually no charge is made for viewing. But to see the graphic works of the great masters in any quantity requires a visit to one or more of the important collections. These are too vast to be on permanent display so generally only selected works are on view and a special application is required to see others.

The British Museum Department of Prints and Drawings has more than 100,000 drawings, among which all the dominant Renaissance figures are represented, such as Leonardo da Vinci, Michelangelo, Botticelli and others, as well as the finest of the north European masters – Dürer, Rubens and Rembrandt. The Victoria and Albert Museum Department of Prints and Drawings is similarly blessed with a wide range of Old Master and Modern works on paper. In addition to painted portraits, the National Portrait Gallery owns a great number of portrait drawings of famous British people, many of which are by leading British artists. The superb Royal Collection of master drawings at Windsor Castle includes some 600 by Leonardo da Vinci and a magnificent series of Holbein portraits. Selected works from this collection are occasionally on show at the Queen's Gallery in London.

There are other major collections of drawings by the great masters at the Ashmolean Museum in Oxford, the Fitzwilliam Museum in Cambridge and Chatsworth House in Derbyshire, which has one of the finest private collections in the world.

The most outstanding collection outside Britain can be found in the Cabinet des Dessins in the Louvre in Paris. Other outstanding collections in Europe can be seen at the Teylers Museum in Haarlem, the Musée des Beaux-Arts in Lille, the Uffizi in Florence, and the Albertina in Vienna. In the United States, the Pierpont Morgan Library in New York, the Paul Getty Museum in Malibu, and the Fogg Art Museum at Harvard University have major collections of drawings.

Drawings and other graphic works by past and present leading artists have also been featured in any number of books and catalogues. The larger museums have their own bookshops and most of the larger chains of bookshops have specialist departments for the arts. Catalogues from past exhibitions are well worth buying, or at least looking at. For an overall general history of art and the nude in art there are two titles that stand out from all the others: *The Story of Art* by E. H. Gombrich and *The Nude* by Kenneth Clark. There are also many magnificent monographs on most of the great draughtsmen in European art.

When looking at the drawings of the Old Masters, it should be remembered that they were principally done as preparatory works for paintings, or occasionally sculptures. Apart from demonstrating superlative technique and showing the struggling thought processes in the creation of a composition, there is very often evidence of those spiritual forces that eventually become manifest in the subsequent painting or sculpture. Great works of art often contain more than visual knowledge and understanding. They are the vehicle through which the artist expresses abstract emotions such as pathos, heroism, triumph and love.

Whatever inspirations are brought away from having seen great master drawings no one should deliberately try to copy a specific technique. Every artist must develop his or her own method of solving the problems that confront them. The history of drawing is evolutionary in that it is possible to tell when, where and by whom any single piece of work was done. Although there have been mistakes in attributions where groups of artists have worked closely together, there is never any real doubt as to the time and place where they were originally executed. Period and place have a profound affect on style and content.

In Conclusion

All the suggestions in this book are intended to stimulate participants in the Life Class to see more and more clearly the wonderful and exciting images in front of them. The levels of understanding that are revealed are directly related to the labour that is put in. The more effort you invest, the greater will be the return. The most important message of all is that you should enjoy the quest.

No, madam, there is nothing ugly; I never saw an ugly thing in my life: for let the form of an object be what it may – light, shade, and perspective will always make it beautiful.

John Constable, responding to a woman's criticism of an engraving

The tree which moves some to tears of joy is in the eyes of others only a green thing which stands in the way . . . As a man is, so he sees.

William Blake

> To see a world in a grain of sand
> And a heaven in a wild flower,
> Hold infinity in the palm of your hand
> And eternity in an hour.

William Blake from 'Auguries of Innocence'

Index

The figures in *italics* refer to illustrations.